Learning Microsoft Azure Storage

Build large-scale, real-world apps by effectively planning, deploying, and implementing Azure Storage solutions

Mohamed Waly

BIRMINGHAM - MUMBAI

Learning Microsoft Azure Storage

First published: November 2017

Production reference: 1131117

Published by Packt Publishing Ltd.
Livery Place
35 Livery Street
Birmingham
B3 2PB, UK.
ISBN 978-1-78588-491-7

www.packtpub.com

Credits

Author
Mohamed Waly

Reviewers
Stefano Demiliani
Bert Wolters
Sjoukje Zaal

Commissioning Editor
Vijin Boricha

Acquisition Editor
Rahul Nair

Content Development Editors
Sweeny Dias
Nithin Varghese

Technical Editor
Komal Karne

Copy Editor
Safis Editing

Project Coordinator
Virginia Dias

Proofreader
Safis Editing

Indexer
Pratik Shirodkar

Graphics
Tania Dutta

Production Coordinator
Melwyn Dsa

About the Author

Mohamed Waly has shown interest in IT since he was a student. The journey began in 2011 when he joined the college of computer science where he started learning how to work with Windows Server 2008 and was the youngest among his colleagues at the college to achieve certification. In 2012, he joined one of the greatest and most well-known student programs in the world, the Microsoft Student Partner program. During the time he spent on the program, he took many communication and presentation skills sessions that helped him to deliver many sessions since his second year at college and the journey continues until now. In the meantime, Waly learned some other topics such as Exchange Server System Center, VMware vSphere, and Microsoft Azure, formerly known as Windows Azure.

He has worked in multiple communities, such as the Azure Community in Egypt, and the Open Source on Azure. Also, he served multiple internships during his time in the university to improve his experience. That's why, in July 2014, Microsoft recognized Mohamed Waly as the youngest MVP in the world. After finishing college, he worked for two of the biggest Microsoft Partners in Egypt—Global Knowledge and Blue Cloud Technologies—as a system engineer and an associate infrastructure consultant, respectively, serving Microsoft Customers in the EMEA region by designing and implementing virtualization and Cloud solutions.

This book would not have seen the light without the help of many people. First, I'd like to thank the team at Packt, which includes Rahul Nair, Sweeny Dias, Komal Karne, Nithin George, and every member of staff from Packt who has helped in producing the book in that manner.

Of course, the technical reviews Bert Wolters, Sjoukje Zaal, and Demiliani Stefano have added great value to the book. I'd like to thank them for their endless support.

Last but not least, I'd like to thank my teammates at Blue Cloud Technologies for sharing their experience with me all the time and their guidance along the way: Moataz Shaaban, Karim Hamdy, Mohamed Saeed, and Emad Samir. I really consider them as a blessing and my second family.

About the Reviewers

Stefano Demiliani is a Microsoft Certified Solution Developer (MCSD), MCSA, MCAD, MCTS on Microsoft Dynamics NAV, MCTS on SharePoint, MCTS on SQL Server and a longtime expert on other Microsoft-related technologies. He has a master's degree in computer engineering from Politecnico of Turin.

Currently, he works as a senior project manager and solution architect for EID, a company of Navlab group, one of the biggest Microsoft Dynamics groups in Italy (where he's also the chief technical officer). His main task is architecting and developing enterprise solutions based on the entire stack of Microsoft technologies (Microsoft Dynamics NAV, Microsoft SharePoint, Azure, cloud apps and .NET applications in general, data analysis, and BI solutions) and he's often focused on engineering distributed service-based applications. He works as a full-time NAV consultant (with more than 15 years of international NAV projects) and solution developer and he is available for architecting solutions based on the Microsoft's ERP, for NAV database tuning and optimization (performance and locking management) and for architecting cloud solutions and apps. He's the author of different Microsoft Certified for NAV add-ons.

Stefano writes many articles and blogs on different Microsoft-related topics and he's frequently involved in consulting and teaching. He has worked with Packt in the past on many technical Microsoft-related books and he's recently the author of *Building ERP Solutions with Microsoft Dynamics NAV*, a book about enterprise solution development with the NAV ERP, Azure Cloud services, and Microsoft technologies. In its free time, Stefano is a runner and a cyclist.

Bert Wolters is currently a lead consultant in hybrid datacenter at the Dutch company Inspark. Bert started his professional life in the Dutch Military, but around 1999 found his talents to be in IT, helping out the platoon and unit leaders with small IT issues in the field. By the time he started on his first Microsoft certification in 2005, he had found his new vocation in life. His ability to look at all sides of a story (issues/problems, solutions, and implementation), was formed by the wide variety of jobs he took. Having a background in the business side of IT as well as Incident and Change Manager, and in the field as engineer and consultant, helps him deliver the most comprehensive solutions for businesses whether technology or business-case driven.

Since 2010, he further specialized in Microsoft infrastructure technology, focusing on system and platform management and is still riding Microsoft's wave of innovation, looking forward to, and experimenting with, every single new infrastructure feature of Microsoft Azure. Because of this focus, he decided to resign from the Dutch PowerShell User Group (DuPSUg), and the System Center User Group in The Netherlands (SCUG_NL), and chair the Experts Live Foundation.

He currently advises companies on how to get the most out of their Azure platform implementation or System Center Suite and provides knowledge on Microsoft's hybrid cloud, Hyper-V, Azure Stack, Microsoft OMS, and StorSimple.

I would like to thank my girlfriend and daughters for putting up with all of my efforts to gain and share knowledge. I also give thanks to Mohamed Waly for accepting me in his team of reviewers.

Sjoukje Zaal is a Microsoft Azure MVP, a Principal Architect and Lead Productivity and with over 15 years of experience providing architecture, development, consultancy, and design expertise. She works at Ordina, a system integrator based in the Netherlands. She is very active in the Microsoft community as co-founder of SP&C NL and MixUG, writer, public speaker and on MSDN/TechNet.

www.PacktPub.com

For support files and downloads related to your book, please visit www.PacktPub.com. Did you know that Packt offers eBook versions of every book published, with PDF and ePub files available? You can upgrade to the eBook version at www.PacktPub.com and as a print book customer, you are entitled to a discount on the eBook copy. Get in touch with us at service@packtpub.com for more details.

At www.PacktPub.com, you can also read a collection of free technical articles, sign up for a range of free newsletters and receive exclusive discounts and offers on Packt books and eBooks.

https://www.packtpub.com/mapt

Get the most in-demand software skills with Mapt. Mapt gives you full access to all Packt books and video courses, as well as industry-leading tools to help you plan your personal development and advance your career.

Why subscribe?

- Fully searchable across every book published by Packt
- Copy and paste, print, and bookmark content
- On demand and accessible via a web browser

Customer Feedback

Thanks for purchasing this Packt book. At Packt, quality is at the heart of our editorial process. To help us improve, please leave us an honest review on this book's Amazon page at `https://www.amazon.com/dp/1785884913`.

If you'd like to join our team of regular reviewers, you can email us at `customerreviews@packtpub.com`. We award our regular reviewers with free eBooks and videos in exchange for their valuable feedback. Help us be relentless in improving our products!

Table of Contents

Preface

First off, I'd like to thank you for purchasing *Learning Microsoft Azure Storage*. Throughout the book, I've shared my entire experience with Azure Storage, which started in 2012 and has witnessed many changes in the storage services.

Microsoft Azure Storage is the bedrock of Microsoft's core storage solution offering in Azure. No matter what solution you are building for the cloud, you'll find a compelling use for Azure Storage. This book will help you get up-to-speed quickly with Microsoft Azure Storage by teaching you how to use the different storage services. You will be able to leverage secure design patterns based on real-world scenarios and develop a strong storage foundation for Azure Virtual Machines, and even your on-premises environment. The aim of this book is to provide accurate and easy-to-follow instructions when working with Azure Storage.

I hope that this book will be a great asset to you. Also, if you have any questions, comments, or suggestions, you can post it in the author online forum.

What this book covers

Chapter 1, *Understanding Azure Storage 101*, introduces Azure Storage and its types. It helps you understand the difference between Azure Service Management (ASM), Azure Resource Management (ARM) model, and Azure Storage types in addition to working with Azure Storage accounts and using PowerShell to automate some, such as creating a storage account.

Chapter 2, *Delving into Azure Storage*, introduces Azure Storage services and explains how to work with them. It will also cover the architecture of Azure Storage and how to secure Azure Storage services, and the best practices that need to be followed to design highly available applications and the role of client libraries with storage services.

Chapter 3, *Azure Storage for VMs*, covers the process of creating Azure VMs and how it relates to and depend on Azure Storage, followed by the best practices you need to know to create a better and more cost-effective design for Azure VMs.

Chapter 4, *Implementing Azure SQL Databases*, introduces Azure SQL Databases and why to use them. The services tier and performance levels will also be covered followed by how to create, and restore Azure SQL Databases.

Chapter 5, *Beyond Azure SQL Database Management*, covers how the SQL database works in the (IaaS/PaaS) service model, how to work with elastic database pools, integrate Azure AD with Azure SQL Database, and how to make sure that your databases will be up and running even in the event that disasters occur.

Chapter 6, *Azure Backup*, introduces Azure Backup and why it is so important to use, how to configure it and how to go through the restoration process.

Chapter 7, *Azure Site Recovery*, introduces Azure Site Recovery and why to work with it. Then we move on to how to prepare your environment for Azure Site Recovery, how to implement it, and even test whether it works or not.

Chapter 8, *Extending Your Azure Storage Management*, covers StorSimple which is used to spread your storage across on-premises and Azure Storage, and some other cool tools, such as AzCopy and Azure Storage Explorer. Finally, you will be introduced to Azure Storage's three musketeers: monitoring, diagnosing, and troubleshooting.

What you need for this book

To follow along with what is covered in the book, you do not need a lot of resources. You only need a Windows 8 or above/Windows Server 2008 R2 or above for most of the topics with Azure PowerShell module installed on it, a SQL Server Management Studio 17.3 to connect to Azure SQL Database, as well as a quad-core, 8 GB memory, and 500 GB Disk VM to be used while working with Azure Site Recovery and StorSimple. Finally, some simple tools, such as AzCopy and Azure Storage Explorer would need to be downloaded.

Who this book is for

This book is intended at anyone interested in Azure generally, and Azure Storage specifically. Some basic knowledge about Azure, Hyper-V, and SQL Server would be very beneficial, but it is not mandatory.

Conventions

In this book, you will find a number of text styles that distinguish between different kinds of information. Here are some examples of these styles and an explanation of their meaning. Code words in text, database table names, folder names, filenames, file extensions, pathnames, dummy URLs, user input, and Twitter handles are shown as follows: "Click on **More services** and a new blade will open. In the search bar, write storage account." A block of code is set as follows:

```
$Subnet = New-AzureRmVirtualNetworkSubnetConfig -Name PacktPubSubnet -
AddressPrefix 10.0.0.0/24
$VirtualNetwork = New-AzureRmVirtualNetwork -ResourceGroupName PacktPub -
Location WestEurope -Name PacktPubvNet -AddressPrefix 10.0.0.0/8 -Subnet
$Subnet
```

Any command-line input or output is written as follows:

```
az storage container create --name packtpubbs --public-access container --
account-name packtpubsacli
```

New terms and **important words** are shown in bold. Words that you see on the screen, for example, in menus or dialog boxes, appear in the text like this: "To upload files to it, click on **Upload** and browse for the desired file."

 Warnings or important notes appear like this.

 Tips and tricks appear like this.

Reader feedback

Feedback from our readers is always welcome. Let us know what you think about this book-what you liked or disliked. Reader feedback is important for us as it helps us develop titles that you will really get the most out of. To send us general feedback, simply email feedback@packtpub.com, and mention the book's title in the subject of your message. If there is a topic that you have expertise in and you are interested in either writing or contributing to a book, see our author guide at www.packtpub.com/authors.

Customer support

Now that you are the proud owner of a Packt book, we have a number of things to help you to get the most from your purchase.

Downloading the color images of this book

We also provide you with a PDF file that has color images of the screenshots/diagrams used in this book. The color images will help you better understand the changes in the output. You can download this file from `https://www.packtpub.com/sites/default/files/downloads/LearningMicrosoftAzureStorage_ColorImages.pdf`.

Errata

Although we have taken every care to ensure the accuracy of our content, mistakes do happen. If you find a mistake in one of our books-maybe a mistake in the text or the code-we would be grateful if you could report this to us. By doing so, you can save other readers from frustration and help us improve subsequent versions of this book. If you find any errata, please report them by visiting `http://www.packtpub.com/submit-errata`, selecting your book, clicking on the **Errata Submission Form** link, and entering the details of your errata. Once your errata are verified, your submission will be accepted and the errata will be uploaded to our website or added to any list of existing errata under the Errata section of that title. To view the previously submitted errata, go to `https://www.packtpub.com/books/content/support` and enter the name of the book in the search field. The required information will appear under the **Errata** section.

Piracy

Piracy of copyrighted material on the internet is an ongoing problem across all media. At Packt, we take the protection of our copyright and licenses very seriously. If you come across any illegal copies of our works in any form on the internet, please provide us with the location address or website name immediately so that we can pursue a remedy. Please contact us at `copyright@packtpub.com` with a link to the suspected pirated material. We appreciate your help in protecting our authors and our ability to bring you valuable content.

Questions

If you have a problem with any aspect of this book, you can contact us at `questions@packtpub.com`, and we will do our best to address the problem.

1

Understanding Azure Storage 101

This chapter introduces Microsoft Azure Storage, its types, and the differences between Azure's different models. It also introduces Azure Storage accounts and how to work with them. Moreover, you will have learned how to automate all of these tasks by the end of the chapter.

The following topics will be covered:

- An introduction to Microsoft Azure Storage
- Why Azure Storage?
- Azure terminologies
- **Azure Service Management** (**ASM**) versus the **Azure Resource Manager** (**ARM**) model
- Azure Storage types
- Azure Storage accounts
- Automating Azure tasks

An introduction to Microsoft Azure Storage

Storage has always been one of the most important cornerstones of every system. You cannot imagine a **virtual machine** (**VM**), web application, or mobile application running without any sort of dependency on storage, and that is what we will cover throughout this book, but from the perspective of the cloud generally, and Azure specifically.

Microsoft Azure Storage is the bedrock of Microsoft's core storage solution offering in Azure. No matter what solution you are building for the cloud, you'll find a compelling use for Azure Storage.

Microsoft Azure Storage is not just a traditional storage system; it's scalable and can store up to hundreds of terabytes of data, meaning that it fits almost every scenario you can ever imagine in many fields, such as IT, science, medical fields, and so on.

At the time of writing, Microsoft Azure is generally available in 36 regions, with plans announced for six additional regions, as shown in the following figure:

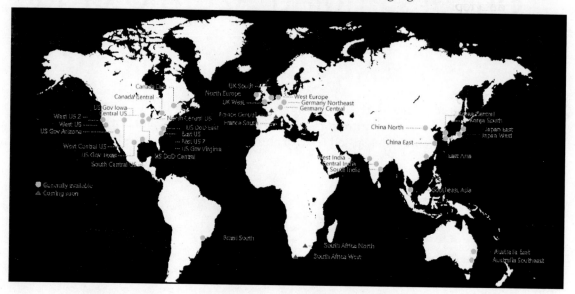

Figure 1.1: Azure regions

This global presence means you can host your storage in the nearest region and access it from anywhere in the world. Considering that Microsoft continues to build new data centers in new regions, the latency between you and your services in Azure will decrease.

 You can find out the nearest region to you with the lowest latency via the following website http://www.azurespeed.com/.

Azure services are available in 140 countries around the globe and supports 17 languages and 24 currencies.

Why Azure Storage?

There are many reasons for using Azure Storage which will be covered throughout this book. Below is a sneak peak of a couple of them:

- **Global presence**: You can host your storage wherever you want in the available Azure regions, allowing you to provide applications close to your user base.
- **Redundancy and recovery:** As mentioned earlier in this chapter, Azure has a global presence which can be leveraged to maintain storage availability using data replication even if a disaster occurs in a region, which will be covered later in this chapter.
- **Many flavors:** Azure Storage has many flavors, based on resiliency, durability, connectivity, performance, and so on, which can be used according to your needs in different scenarios. This will be covered later in this chapter.
- **Pay as you go:** Pay as you go has always been one of the distinguished reasons for using the cloud generally. It is no surprise that Azure Storage supports this model as well.

Terminologies

Due to an overlap of terms and some misperceptions about the ways that Azure Services are delivered, terminology is a sticking point even for people who have been working with the technology for some time. The following table provides accurate but short definitions for terms related to Azure services. These definitions will be expanded upon in detail throughout the book, so don't worry if they are confused at first:

Term	Definition
On-premises	Means that your data center is hosted and managed from within your company.
Off-premises	Means that your data center is hosted and managed in a remote place (for example, hosted and managed outside your company).
Azure VM	The feature of providing VMs to Azure subscribers.
Blade	The window that pops up when you click on one of the Azure services in the Azure portal, such as **Virtual machines**.

Journey	A set of blades or chain of selections. For instance, when you select Virtual Machines inside the Azure Portal, click on an existing virtual machine and then select its settings.
Resource group	Provides a logical container for Azure resources (to help manage resources that are often used together).
Images	The VMs you've created in Azure and then captured to be used as templates for later use, or the VMs you've imported to Azure.
Disks	**Virtual Hard Disks** (**VHDs**) that you attach to the VMs you create in Azure.
Virtual network	Allows VMs and services that are part of the same virtual network to access each other. However, services outside the virtual network have no way of connecting to services hosted within virtual networks unless you decide to do so.
Fault domain	A group of resources that could fail at the same time. For example, they are in the same rack.
Upgrade/update domain	A group of resources that can be updated simultaneously during system upgrades.
Storage container	The place where storage Blobs are stored, it is also used to assign security policies to the Blobs stored inside it.
Network Security Group (**NSG**)	Determines the protocols, ports, who and what can access Azure VMs remotely.
VM agent /extensions	Software components that extend the VM functionality and simplify various management operations.
Scale set	A set of identical VMs, that auto scale without pre-provisioning the VMs based on metrics such as CPU, memory, and so on.
Availability set	When VMs are placed in an availability set, the VMs are spread over different fault domains and update domains, which ensures that, in the event of a rack failure, not all instances are brought down at the same time. If any updates are applied to a host on which there is one of your VMs and a restart is required, it will not be applied to the other VM within the same availability set.

System Preparation (SysPrep)	A Windows preparation tool that's used when you have captured a VM and want to use it as a template, which ensures that there's no more than one VM with the same properties, which would lead to a conflict between the VMs.

ASM versus ARM model

At the time of writing, Azure services are being provided via two portals, which follow two different models. The Azure classic portal follows the ASM model and the Azure portal follows the ARM model.

Azure classic portal (ASM model)

Historically, Azure services were provided via one portal prior to 2014, the classic portal, which can be accessed via the following URL `https://manage.windowsazure.com/`.

The model that was used for that portal is called the **ASM model**, within which each resource existed independently. You could not manage your resources together; you had to build up and track each resource. For example, you would have to manage storage from the storage blade, and the same goes for the virtual networks, VMs, and so on. So, when your environment got bigger, there would be chaos in the management scheme. You would have to know which VMs were stored in which storage account, and that could lead to some critical situations, such as reaching the IOPs limits of the storage account. In turn, this could result in you accidentally creating a new VM and assigning it to that storage account. As a result, the VM would run with terrible performance. This would not be your only concern when working with the ASM model; you might want to delete a solution with multiple resources, which you would have to do manually for each resource.

When you open the Azure classic portal, it will look like the following screenshot:

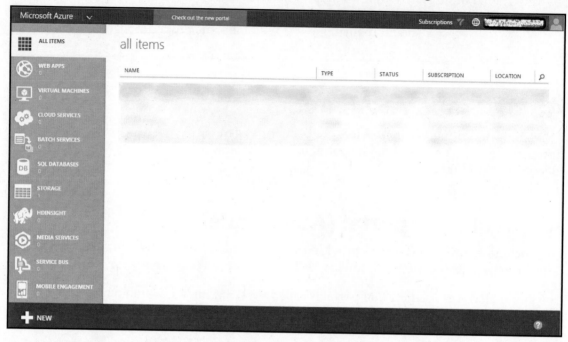

Figure 1.2: Azure classic portal

Azure portal (ARM model)

In 2014, Microsoft launched a new portal which follows a new model, called the **ARM model.** This portal can be accessed via the following URL `https://portal.azure.com/`.

This model depends on the concept of resource groups, which means you can group all your resources within a container, resulting in resources being deployed in parallel. As a result, you will not face the same problems as you did with the classic portal.

The following diagram describes the deployed resources through the ARM model:

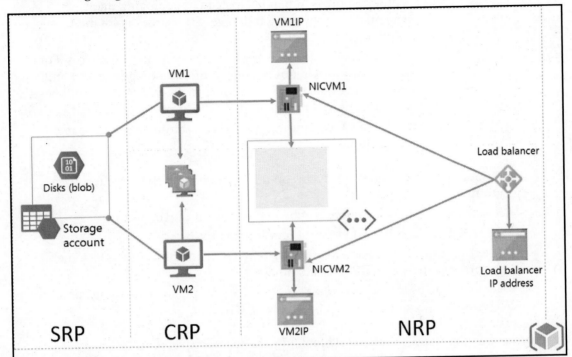

Figure 1.3: Resource Manager management model at a high level

Here are the benefits you will gain using this portal:

- Ability to manage your resources as a group instead of managing them separately.
- Use **Role Based Access Control (RBAC)** to control access to resources, so that you can assign permissions to a user on a resource or some resources but not to other resources (as it was in the classic portal).
- Use tags to organize and classify your resources, which can help you with billing. For example, you might want to monitor the billing of some resources that make up a solution, for example, a web server. By assigning a tag to the resources that make up that solution, you would be able to monitor its billing, and so on.

- Support the usability of JSON to deploy resources instead of using the portal.
  - Deploy resources in parallel instead of deploying them sequentially and waiting until every resource deployment finishes to deploy another one.
  - Specify dependencies during the deployment of resources. For example, a VM will not be created until a storage account and a virtual network are deployed because the VM VHD would need a place to be stored in and an IP Address from a virtual network./li>
  - Reuse the JSON template to deploy a solution with the same specifications.

- Resources with the same life cycle should be gathered in the same resource group.
- Resources in different regions can be in the same resource group.
- The resource cannot exist in multiple resource groups.
- A resource group supports RBAC, wherein a user can have access to some specific resources, but no access to others.
- Some resources can be shared across resource groups, such as storage accounts.
- ARM VMs can only be placed in ARM storage accounts.

When you open the Azure portal, it will look like the following screenshot:

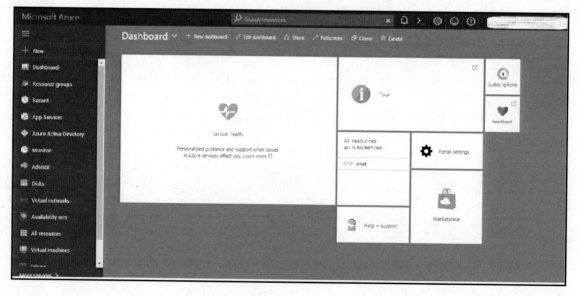

Figure 1.4: Azure portal

- You can change the background of the portal by double-clicking on any unused area of the dashboard. You can navigate between four colors (blue, dark blue, white, and black).
- For further information about the difference between the ARM and ASM models, check out the following article: `https://blogs.technet.microsoft.com/meamcs/2016/12/22/difference-between-azure-service-manager-and-azure-resource-manager/`.

Deployment model tricks

Here are some things you need to consider:

- You cannot create a VM using the ARM model and assign it to a virtual network built using the ASM model
- You cannot use a prebuilt image that was created using ASM APIs to build a VM using the ARM model, but as a workaround, you can copy the VHD files from the storage account in the classic portal to a storage account created in the ARM model
- You can migrate assets from the ASM model to the ARM model
- Every resource must be assigned to a resource group, so whenever you want to move a resource between resource groups you must remove it from its current resource group, then add it to the new resource group.

Azure Storage types

Azure Storage has many types and even subtypes of those types in order to satisfy Azure services' consumer needs and to fit most scenarios.

The most common types can be classified based on the following factors:

- Durability (replication)
- Performance (Standard versus Premium)
- Persistency (persistent versus non-persistent)

Durability

One of the most buzzing questions about the cloud generally is:

What if, for some reason, the SAN/servers that store my data are completely damaged? How can I restore my data?

The answer is very simple because Microsoft Azure Storage is durable and supports data replication, therefore you can make sure your storage is highly available.

Replication ensures that your data is copied somewhere else, whether in the same data center, another data center, or even another region.

 For more info about the SLA of Azure Storage, you can access it via the following link: `https://azure.microsoft.com/en-us/support/legal/sla/storage/v1_2/`.

Replication types

Microsoft Azure supports multiple options for data replication. You can use whatever you feel suits your business, especially as every type has its own price.

In order to calculate your solution's cost, you can use the **Azure Pricing Calculator**, which can be reached via the following URL: `https://azure.microsoft.com/en-us/pricing/calculator/`.

Locally redundant storage

Locally redundant storage (LRS) replicates three copies of your data within the same data center you have your data in. The write requests you do with your storage are not committed until they are replicated to all three copies, which means it replicates synchronously. Not only this, it also makes sure that these three copies exist in different update domains and fault domains. You can revise the terms guide at the beginning of the chapter to understand what the update domain and the fault domain are.

Drawbacks:

- The least durable option, as it replicates only within the same data center
- Your data will be lost if a catastrophic event, such as a volcanic eruption or flood, affects the data center

Advantages:

- It is the cheapest type compared to the other types
- It is the fastest type of data replication, offering the highest throughput since it replicates within the same data center, mitigating the risk of data loss that would occur during data replication caused by a failure having occurred on the original data host
- It is the only available replication type that can be used with Premium Storage at the time of writing

Zone Redundant Storage

Zone Redundant Storage (ZRS) replicates three copies of data across two or three data centers within one of two regions asynchronously, plus the three copies of data stored within the same data center of the original source of the data.

Drawbacks:

- This type can only be used for Block Blobs (one of the Azure services covered in the next chapter), and a Standard Storage account (general purpose Standard Storage accounts will be covered later in this chapter)
- Does not support metrics or logging
- Does not support conversion for other replication types, such as LRS, GRS, and vice versa
- If a disaster occurs, some data might be lost, because the data replicates to the other data center asynchronously
- If a disaster occurs, there will be some delay in accessing your data until Microsoft failover to the secondary zone

Advantage: It provides higher durability and availability for data than LRS, as it not only replicates in the same data center but also in other data centers.

Geo-redundant storage

Geo-redundant storage (GRS) replicates data not only within the same region but also to another region. Firstly, it replicates three copies of data within the same region synchronously, then it replicates another three copies of data to other regions asynchronously.

Drawbacks:

- If a disaster occurs, some data might be lost, because the data replicates to the other regions asynchronously
- If a disaster occurs, there will be some delay in accessing your data until Microsoft initiates failover to the secondary region

Advantages:

- It provides the highest durability and availability, even if a disaster occurs in an entire region
- Unlike ZRS, if the original source of data faces an outage, there will be no possibility of data loss if the other three copies that exist within the same region don't face an outage too, as it replicates synchronously within the same region.

Read-access geo-redundant storage

Read-access geo-redundant storage (RA-GRS) follows the same replication mechanism of GRS, in addition, to read access on your replicated data in the other regions.

Drawback: If a disaster occurs, some data might be lost, because the data replicates to the other region asynchronously.

Advantages:

- It provides the highest durability and availability, even if a disaster occurs in a whole region
- If a disaster occurs, you still only have read access to the storage, but no write access until Microsoft initiates failover to the secondary region
- The region with the read access can be used for data retrieval by the nearest offices to it without the need to go to another region to access the data; as a result, the data latency will decrease

Regarding replication between different regions, it will not work with just any two regions; the regions must be paired.
For example the West Europe region can replicate with North Europe, and not any other region.
For more information about paired regions, check the following article:
`https://docs.microsoft.com/en-us/azure/best-practices-availability-paired-regions`.

Performance

As mentioned earlier, Azure provides services for all business types and needs. There are two types based on Azure Storage performance--Standard and Premium.

Standard Storage

Standard Storage is the most common type for all the VMs sizes available in Azure. The Standard Storage type stores its data on non-SSD disks. It is commonly used with workloads within which the latency is not critical. Plus, it is low cost and has support for all Azure Storage services (which will be covered in the next chapter). It is also available in all regions.

Premium Storage

Premium Storage is designed for low latency applications, such as SQL server, which needs intensive IOPs. Premium Storage is stored on SSD disks, that is why it costs more than Standard Storage. Microsoft recommends using Premium Storage for better performance and higher availability.

 More details about Standard and Premium Storage will be covered throughout the book.

Persistency

Another type of Azure Storage depends on data persistence, which means whether data will be there or not after stopping and starting the VM within which your data exists.

Persistent storage

Persistent storage means that the data will be there after stopping and restarting the VM within which your data exists.

Non-persistent storage

Non-persistent storage means that the data will be gone after restarting the VM within which your data exists.

 Further details about storage persistency will be covered in `Chapter 3,` *Azure Storage for VMs*.

Azure Storage accounts

An Azure Storage account is a secure account that provides access to Azure Storage services (which will be covered in the next chapter), and a unique namespace for storage resources.

During the creation of a new Azure Storage account, you will have the option to choose one of two kinds of storage accounts:

- General-purpose storage account
- Blob storage account

General-purpose storage accounts

A general-purpose storage account gives you access to all Azure Storage services, such as Blobs, Tables, Files, and Queues (these will be covered in the next chapter), and has two performance tiers:

- Standard Storage tier
- Premium Storage tier

Both were covered within the *Performance* type topic earlier in this chapter.

Blob storage accounts

Unlike a general-purpose storage account, not all Azure Storage services are meant to be stored in a Blob storage account because they are dedicated to storing unstructured data. Therefore, a Blob storage service is the only type allowed to be accessed by a Blob storage account. However, it only supports block and appends Blobs.

A Blob storage account has a usage pattern called access tiers, which determines how frequently you access your data and based on that you will get billed.

Currently, there are two types:

- Hot access tier
- Cool access tier

Hot access tier

With the hot access tier, objects will be accessed more frequently, so you will pay less for data access, but pay more for data size.

Cool access tier

With the cool access tier, objects will be accessed less frequently, so you will pay more for data access, but less for data size.

Azure Storage Account tips

The following tips will increase your knowledge about Azure Storage, and will definitely help you when you want to design a storage solution on Azure:

- You cannot switch between an Azure general-purpose storage account and an Azure Blob storage account
- You can switch between access tiers with a Blob storage account, but with the possibility of additional charges being incurred
- A Blob storage account does not support ZRS replication type at the time of writing
- Premium Storage only supports Locally Redundant Storage as a replication type at the time of writing
- Premium Storage is not supported for a Blob storage account at the time of writing
- Azure supports up to 200 storage accounts per subscription by default
- A storage account can store data up to 500 TB

- Azure Storage supports encryption for only two storage services at the time of writing (Blobs and Files), and you can enable it during the storage account creation
- If you are using REST APIs to connect to Azure Storage, you can secure the transfer by enabling that option during the creation of a storage account
- Only lowercase letters and numbers are supported for the name of the storage account

Creating an Azure Storage account

Let's get our hands dirty with creating a storage account with the following parameters:

- **Name:** `packtpubsa`
- **Deployment model:** Resource Manager
- **Account kind: General purpose**
- **Performance: Standard**
- **Replication: Locally-redundant storage (LRS)**
- **Storage service encryption (blobs and files): Disabled**
- **Secure transfer required: Disabled**
- **Subscription:** Select the right subscription for this task
- **Resource group:** Create a new or select an existing resource group, as per your needs
- **Location:** Select the nearest location to you

Without further ado, let's get started:

1. Open the Azure portal from here: `https://portal.azure.com/`.

2. Click on **More services** and a new blade will open. In the search bar, write `storage account`, as shown in the following screenshot:

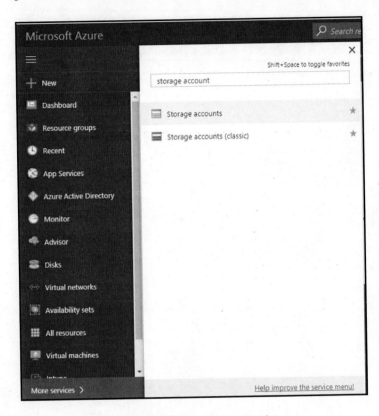

Figure 1.5: Searching for a storage accounts service

3. Click on **Storage accounts** and a new blade will open. Click on **Add**, as shown in the following screenshot:

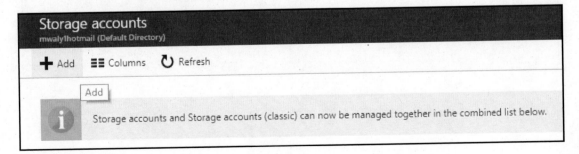

Figure 1.6: Adding a new storage account

4. A new blade will open, wherein you need to fill in the fields and determine the types as per your needs:

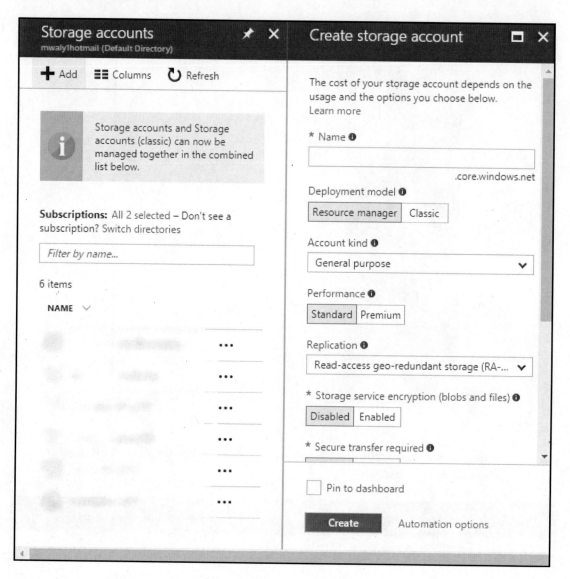

Figure 1.7: Creating a new storage account blade

5. Fill in the fields as before, and click on **Create**:

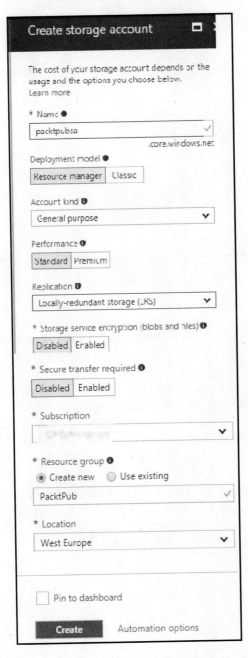

Figure 1.8: Filling in the fields of the blade

6. Once done, you can find your storage account in the **Storage accounts** blade:

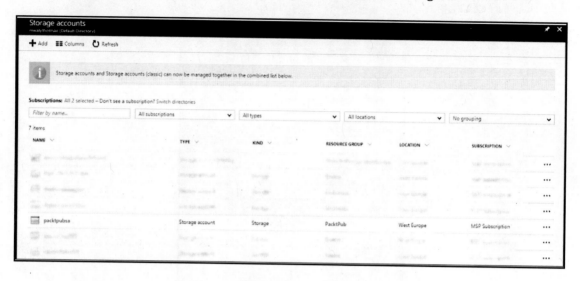

Figure 1.9: Storage accounts blade

Something to keep in mind:

- When using **Storage service encryption (blobs and files)**, your data is encrypted once it is written in Azure and gets decrypted once you try to access it.

- When you enable **Secure transfer required**, the storage account will only be accessed using HTTPS if you are using REST APIs, and since Azure file service uses **Server Message Block (SMB)**, the connection will fail if you are using SMB 2.1 and SMB 3.0 without encryption, and the same goes for the Linux SMB client in some flavors.

- When you enable **Secure transfer required**, you will not be able to use a custom domain, because Azure Storage does not currently support that. As a result, you can only use the default `.core.windows.net` domain.

Automating your tasks

It is no surprise that we commonly face repetitive and time-consuming tasks. For example, you might want to create multiple storage accounts. You would have to follow the previous guide multiple times to get your job done. This is why Microsoft supports its Azure services with multiple ways of automating most of the tasks that can be implemented in Azure. Throughout this book, two of the automation methods that Azure supports will be used.

Azure PowerShell

PowerShell is commonly used with most Microsoft products, and Azure is no less important than these products.

Mainly, you can use Azure PowerShell cmdlets to manage your Azure Storage, however, you should be aware that Microsoft Azure has two types of cmdlets: one for the classic portal, and another for the portal we are using.

The main difference between the cmdlets of the classic portal and the current portal is there will be an RM added to the cmdlet of the current portal.

For example, if you want to create a storage account in the classic portal, you would use the following cmdlet:

```
New-AzureStorageAccount
```

But for the current portal, you would use:

```
New-AzureRMStorageAccount
```

By default, you can use Azure PowerShell cmdlets in Windows PowerShell; you will have to install its module first.

Installing the Azure PowerShell module

There are two ways to install the Azure PowerShell module:

- Download and install the module from the following link: `https://www.microsoft.com/web/downloads/platform.aspx`
- Install the module from the PowerShell Gallery

Installing the Azure PowerShell module from the PowerShell Gallery

1. Open PowerShell in elevated mode.
2. To install the Azure PowerShell module for the current portal, run the `Install-Module AzureRM` cmdlet. If your PowerShell requires the NuGet provider, you will be asked to agree to install it and you will have to agree to the installation policy modification, as the repository is not available on your environment, as shown in the following screenshot:

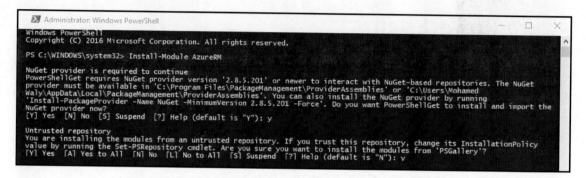

Figure 1.10: Installing the AzureRM PowerShell module

Creating a storage account in the Azure portal using PowerShell

1. Log in to your Azure account using the `Login-AzureRmAccount` cmdlet. You will be prompted to enter your account credentials:

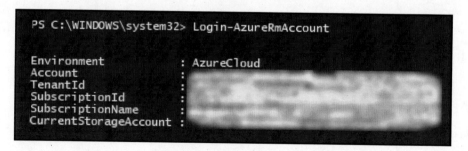

Figure 1.11: Log in to Azure via PowerShell

2. Create another storage account with the same properties as we used for the portal, but with a different name:

```
PS C:\WINDOWS\system32> New-AzureRmStorageAccount -ResourceGroupName "PacktPub" -AccountName "packtpubsaps" -Location "West Europe" -SkuName "Standard_LRS"

ResourceGroupName       : packtpub
StorageAccountName      : packtpubsaps
Id                      : /subscriptions/██████████████████████/resourceGroups/packtpub/providers/Microsoft.Sto
                          rage/storageAccounts/packtpubsaps
Location                : westeurope
Sku                     : Microsoft.Azure.Management.Storage.Models.Sku
Kind                    : Storage
Encryption              :
AccessTier              :
CreationTime            : 7/31/2017 10:08:59 AM
CustomDomain            :
Identity                :
LastGeoFailoverTime     :
PrimaryEndpoints        : Microsoft.Azure.Management.Storage.Models.Endpoints
PrimaryLocation         : westeurope
ProvisioningState       : Succeeded
SecondaryEndpoints      :
SecondaryLocation       :
StatusOfPrimary         : Available
StatusOfSecondary       :
Tags                    : {}
EnableHttpsTrafficOnly  : False
Context                 : Microsoft.WindowsAzure.Commands.Common.Storage.LazyAzureStorageContext
ExtendedProperties      : {}
```

Figure 1.12: Creating a new storage account using PowerShell

3. Congratulations! You have created a storage account using PowerShell.

Azure command-line interface

The Azure **command-line interface (CLI)** is open source, cross-platform, and supports implementing all the tasks you can do in the Azure portal with commands.

Azure CLI comes in two flavors:

- Azure CLI 2.0, which only supports the current Azure portal
- Azure CLI 1.0, which supports both portals

Throughout the book, we will be using Azure CLI 2.0. So, let's get started with its installation.

Installing the Azure CLI 2.0

To understand what the Azure CLI 2.0 is capable of, we need to install it. Let's do so by following these steps:

1. Download Azure CLI 2.0 from the following link: `https://azurecliprod.blob.core.windows.net/msi/azure-cli-2.0.12.msi`.

2. Once downloaded, you can start the installation by following the screenshots shown here:

    1. Run the executable files as administrator, and once the wizard opens, click on **Install**:

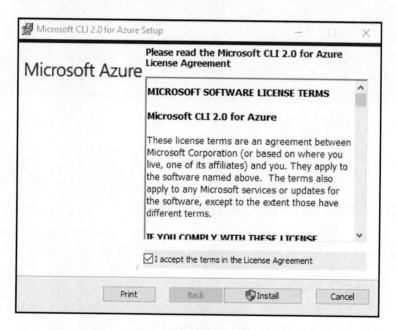

Figure 1.13: Installing the Azure CLI 2.0

    2. Once you click on **Install**, it will start to validate your environment to check whether it is compatible with it or not, then it starts the installation:

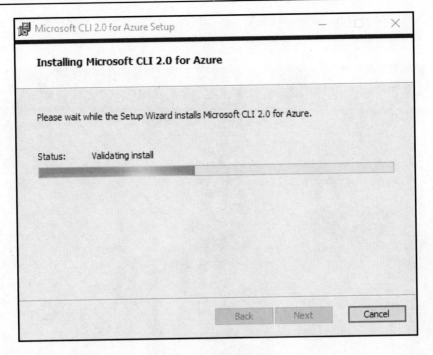

Figure 1.14: Installing Azure CLI 2.0

3. Once the installation completes, you can click on **Finish**, and you are good to go:

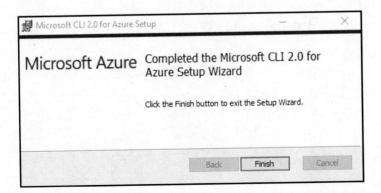

Figure 1.15: Installing Azure CLI 2.0

3. Once done, you can open the cmd and type `az` to access Azure CLI commands, as shown in the following diagram:

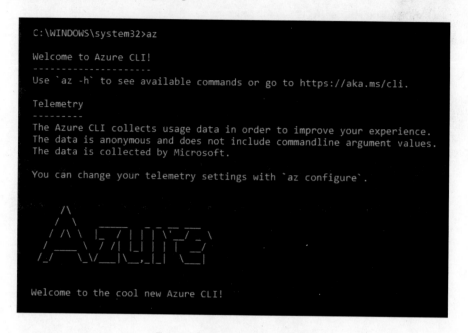

```
C:\WINDOWS\system32>az

Welcome to Azure CLI!
---------------------
Use `az -h` to see available commands or go to https://aka.ms/cli.

Telemetry
---------
The Azure CLI collects usage data in order to improve your experience.
The data is anonymous and does not include commandline argument values.
The data is collected by Microsoft.

You can change your telemetry settings with `az configure`.


       /\
      /  \    _____   _ _  ___ _
     / /\ \  |_  / | | | \'__/ _\
    / ____ \  / /| |_| | | |  __/
   /_/    \_\/___|\__,_|_|  \___|


Welcome to the cool new Azure CLI!
```

Figure 1.16: Opening the Azure CLI using CMD

Creating a Storage account using the Azure CLI 2.0

Let's get our hands dirty with the Azure CLI 2.0 to create an Azure Storage account:

1. Log in to your Azure account using the `az login` command. You have to open the URL that pops up on the CLI and enter the code, as shown in the following screenshot:

```
C:\WINDOWS\system32>az login
To sign in, use a web browser to open the page https://aka.ms/devicelogin and enter the code ████████ to authenticate.
[
  {
    "cloudName": "AzureCloud",
    "id": "████████████████████",
    "isDefault": true,
    "name": "████████████",
    "state": "Enabled",
    "tenantId": "██████████████████████",
    "user": {
      "name": "██████████████",
      "type": "user"
    }
  },
  {
    "cloudName": "AzureCloud",
    "id": "████████████████████",
    "isDefault": false,
    "name": "████████████",
    "state": "Enabled",
    "tenantId": "██████████████████",
    "user": {
      "name": "██████████████",
      "type": "user"
    }
  }
]
C:\WINDOWS\system32>
```

Figure 1.17: Logging in to Azure via the Azure CLI 2.0

2. Create another storage account with the same properties as we used for the portal, but with a different name, as shown in the following screenshot:

```
C:\WINDOWS\system32>az storage account create --location "West Europe" --name packtpubsacli --resource-group "PacktPub"
--sku "Standard_LRS"
{/ Finished ..
  "accessTier": null,
  "creationTime": "2017-07-31T11:14:18.249342+00:00",
  "customDomain": null,
  "enableHttpsTrafficOnly": false,
  "encryption": null,
  "id": "/subscriptions/██████████████████/resourceGroups/packtpub/providers/Microsoft.Storage/storage
Accounts/packtpubsacli",
  "kind": "Storage",
  "lastGeoFailoverTime": null,
  "location": "westeurope",
  "name": "packtpubsacli",
  "primaryEndpoints": {
    "blob": "https://packtpubsacli.blob.core.windows.net/",
    "file": "https://packtpubsacli.file.core.windows.net/",
    "queue": "https://packtpubsacli.queue.core.windows.net/",
    "table": "https://packtpubsacli.table.core.windows.net/"
  },
  "primaryLocation": "westeurope",
  "provisioningState": "Succeeded",
  "resourceGroup": "packtpub",
  "secondaryEndpoints": null,
  "secondaryLocation": null,
  "sku": {
    "name": "Standard_LRS",
    "tier": "Standard"
  },
  "statusOfPrimary": "available",
  "statusOfSecondary": null,
  "tags": {},
  "type": "Microsoft.Storage/storageAccounts"
}
```

Figure 1.18: Creating an Azure storage account using the Azure CLI 2.0

Summary

So far, we have covered some preliminary subject matters regarding Azure generally, and Azure Storage specifically. Some things were not covered in detail, but detailed discussions will be raised in the coming chapters.

Next, Azure Storage architecture and Azure services will be covered in detail. Therefore, the knowledge gained in this chapter is required for a better understanding of the coming chapter.

2
Delving into Azure Storage

This chapter covers Microsoft Azure Storage services and how to work with them. For a better understanding of what is going on behind the scenes, the Azure Storage architecture and how to secure your Azure Storage will be covered too. The best practices that need to be followed to have a highly available application are also covered. Then, we will go through client libraries, which can be used as a way of managing Azure Storage. Finally, all manually created tasks will be automated using PowerShell and the Azure CLI 2.0.

The following topics will be covered in this chapter:

- Azure Storage services
- Understanding the Azure Storage architecture
- Securing Azure Storage
- Storage design for highly available applications
- Understanding client libraries
- Automating tasks

Azure Storage services

Azure Storage has multiple services that would fit most scenarios. At the moment, there are four types of Azure Storage services, which are as follows:

- Blob storage
- Table storage
- Queue storage
- File storage

Each of these services can be used for different scenarios, which we will cover in detail shortly.

Blob storage

Blob stands for **binary large object**. This type of service can store almost everything since it stores unstructured data, such as documents, files, images, VHDs, and so on.

Using the Azure Blob storage service makes you capable of storing everything we have just mentioned, and able to access them from anywhere using different access methods, such as URLs, REST APIs, or even one of the Azure SDK Storage Client Libraries, which will be covered later in this chapter.

There are three types of Blob storage:

- **Block blobs**: They are an excellent choice to store media files, documents, backups, and so on. They are good for files that are read from A-Z (sequential reading).
- **Page blobs**: They support random access for files stored on them, that is why, they are commonly used for storing VHDs of Azure Virtual Machines.
- **Append blobs**: They are similar to block blobs, but are commonly used for append operations. For example, each time a new block is created, it will be added to the end of the blob. One of the most common use cases within which append blobs can be used is logging, where you have multiple threads that need to be written to the same blob. This is an excellent solution that would help you to dump the logs in a fast and safe way.

Creating Blob storage

Let's see how we can create Blob storage that everyone has read/write access to in the storage account we created in the last chapter.

1. Navigate to the storage we created in the last chapter using the portal, as shown in the following screenshot:

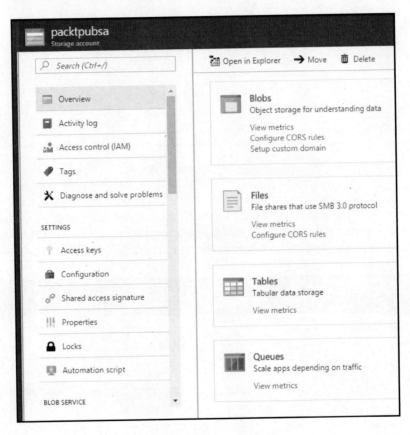

Figure 2.1: Azure Storage services overview

2. You can see all the storage services in the previous screenshot. To manage blobs, you have to click on **Blobs**, and a new blade will appear, as shown in the following screenshot:

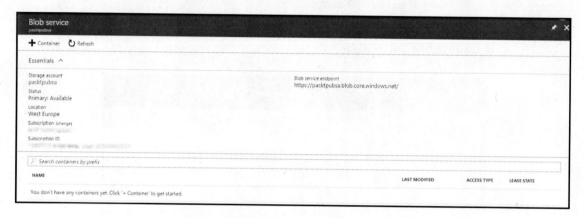

Figure 2.2: Azure Blob service overview

3. In order to create a blob service, you have to create a container in which the blob service will be stored. To do this, you click on **Container** to create a new one. However, it is not a straightforward creation process, as you will be asked to specify a name and an access type, as shown in the following screenshot:

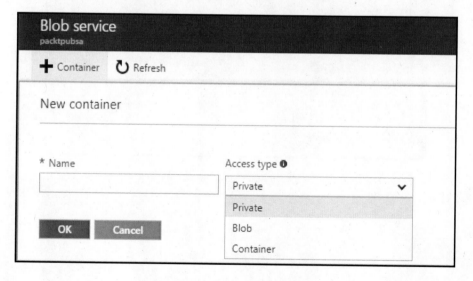

Figure 2.3: Creating a blob service

Here is a short description for the access types:

- **Private**: This option means that only the storage account owner has access to the blobs created within this container using the access key, therefore you can grant access privileges to any other users
- **Blob**: This option means that the blobs created within this container will be accessed from outside by read permissions only
- **Container**: This option means that the blobs created within the container will be publicly available with read and write access

4. Since we want to create a blob service that everyone has read/write access to, we will choose **Access type** as **Container** and name it `packtpubbs`, as shown in the following screenshot:

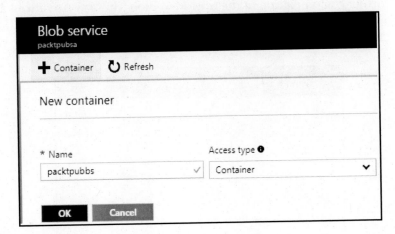

Figure 2.4: Creating a blob service

The access type of storage containers can be changed even after creation.

5. Once created, you can open the blob and start uploading your data to it, as shown in the following screenshot:

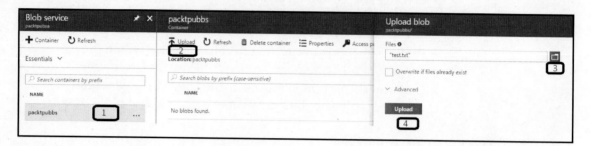

Figure 2.5: Uploading a .txt file to the blob

6. For further customization of the uploaded blob, click on **Advanced** and you will see options such as specifying the **Blob type**, **Block size**, to which folder it will upload the blob, and so on:

Figure 2.6: Advanced customization to the uploaded blob

Blob storage key points

The following tips should be considered, as they will help you when designing your storage solution using blob services:

- Blob storage supports both standards, but only page blobs support Premium Storage.
- Block blobs are named as such because files larger than 64 MB are uploaded as smaller blocks, then get combined into one final blob.
- You cannot change the type of blob once it has been created.
- Block blobs are named as such because they provide random read/write access to 512-byte pages.
- Page blobs can store up to 8 TB.
- Storage containers built for Blob storage may only contain lowercase letters, hyphens, and numbers, and must begin with a letter or a number, however, the name cannot contain two consecutive hyphens. The name length can vary between 3 to 63 characters.
- The maximum number of blocks in a block blob or append blob is 50,000.
- The maximum size of the block in a block blob is 100 MB. As a result, a block blob can store data of up to 4.75 TB.
- The maximum size of the block in an append blob is 4 MB. As a result, an append blob can store data of up to 195 TB.

Table storage

High availability and scalability are key factors when you want to work with your storage, and that is exactly what is offered by Table storage. Table storage is a Microsoft NoSQL data store that can be used for the massive amount of semi-structured, non-relational data.

Data is stored in tables as a collection of entities, where entities are like rows, and each entity has a primary key and a set of properties, considering that a property is like a column.

The Table storage service is schema-less, therefore multiple entities in the same table may have different properties.

An entity has three properties:

- PartitionKey
- RowKey
- Timestamp

PartitionKey

The PartitionKey is a sequential range of entities that have the same key value. The way that tables are partitioned is to support load balancing across storage nodes, where tables entities are organized by partition. It is considered the first part of an entity's primary key.

It may be a string value with a size of up to 1 KB, and every insert, update, or delete operation must be included in the partition key property.

RowKey

RowKey is the second part of the entity's primary key. It is a unique identifier for the entity, and every entity within the table is uniquely identified by the combination of PartitionKey and RowKey.

Like PartitionKey, it is a string value that may be up to 1 KB, and every insert, update, or delete operation must be included in the RowKey property.

Timestamp

Timestamp is a datetime value, and it is kept on the server side to record when the last modification of the entity occurred.

Every time there is a modification for the entity, the Timestamp value is increased. Considering that this value should not be set on insert or update operations.

Creating Table storage

Let's see how we can create Table storage in the storage account we created in the last chapter:

1. Navigate to the storage we created in the last chapter using the portal, as shown in the following screenshot:

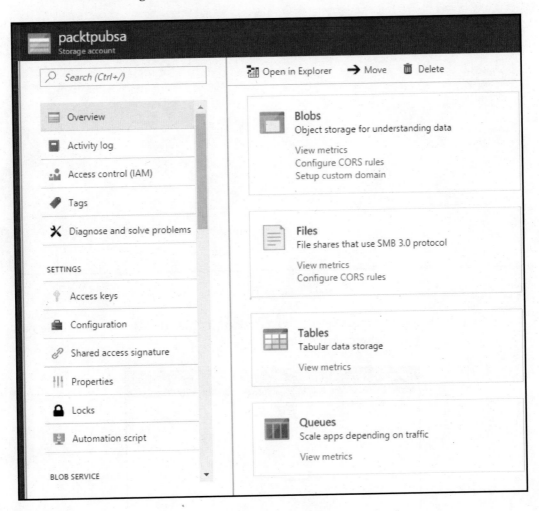

Figure 2.7: Azure Storage services overview

2. You can see all the storage services in the previous screenshot. To manage tables, you have to click on **Tables**, and a new blade will appear, as shown in the following screenshot:

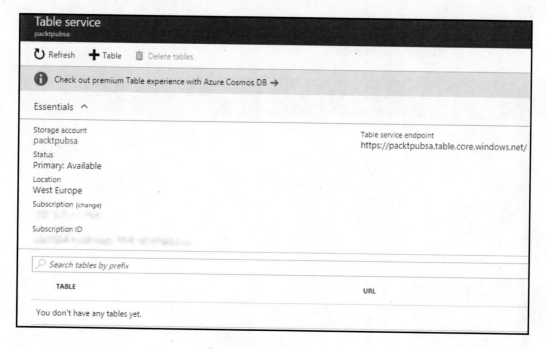

Figure 2.8: Azure Table service overview

3. In order to create a table service, just click on **Table**, and specify the **Table name**, as shown in the following screenshot:

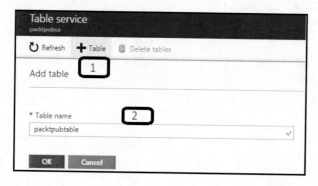

Figure 2.9: Azure Table service creation

4. Once done, you will see that the table has been created, as shown in the following screenshot:

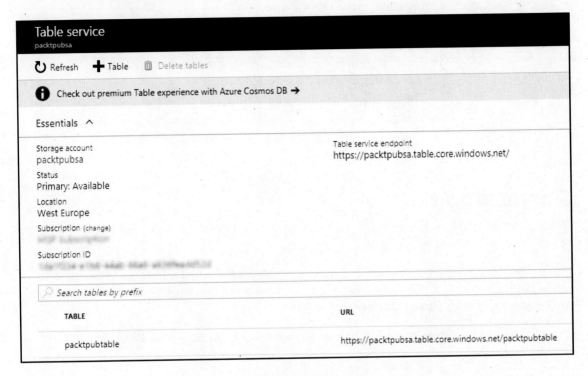

Figure 2.10: The created table

For database developers and administrators who are interested in learning how to access a created table and start working with it, you can check the following link: `https://docs.microsoft.com/en-us/azure/storage/storage-dotnet-how-to-use-tables`.

Table storage key points

The following tips should be considered, as they will help you when designing your storage solution using the Table storage service:

- Table storage supports Standard Storage, but its support for Premium Storage is in preview at the time of writing
- Table storage is significantly lower in cost than traditional SQL

- The entity can have up to 252 custom properties, and 3 system properties (`PartitionKey`, `RowKey`, and `Timestamp`)
- The entity's properties data cannot exceed 1 MB
- Table names must follow the following rules:
    - They are case sensitive
    - They contain only alphanumeric characters, considering that they cannot begin with a numeric character
    - They cannot be redundant within the same storage account
    - You can name a table with another table name written in reverse
    - Their length varies between 3 and 63 characters

Queue storage

Queue storage is a storage service that is used to provide persistent and reliable messaging for application components.

Generally, it creates a list of messages that process asynchronously, following the **First-In, First-Out (FIFO)** model. Not only this, asynchronous tasks and building process workflows can be managed with Queue storage too.

One of the most common scenarios is passing messages from an Azure Web Role to an Azure Worker Role.

Queue storage is not the only messaging solution available at Azure; there are also Service Bus queues, which can be used for more advanced scenarios.

More information about the differences between Azure Queues storage and Azure Service Bus queues, can be found via the following URL: `https://docs.microsoft.com/en-us/azure/service-bus-messaging/service-bus-azure-and-service-bus-queues-compared-contrasted`.

Creating Queue storage

Let's see how we can create Queue storage in the storage account we created in the last chapter.

1. Navigate to the storage we created in the last chapter using the portal, as shown in the following screenshot:

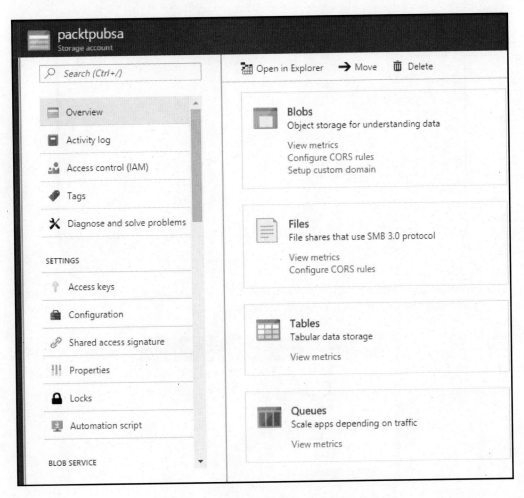

Figure 2.11: Azure Storage services

2. You can see all the storage services in the previous screenshot. To manage queues, you have to click on **Queue**, and a new blade will appear, as shown in the following screenshot:

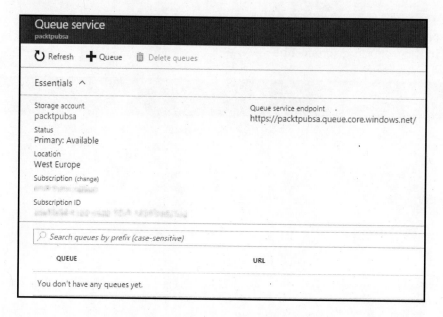

Figure 2.12: Azure Queue service overview

3. In order to create a Queue service, just click on **Queue** and specify the **Queue name**, as shown in the following screenshot:

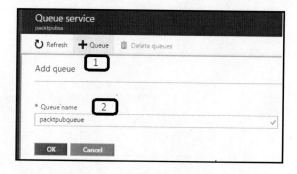

Figure 2.13: Azure Queue service creation

4. Once done, you will see that the Queue has been created, as shown in the following screenshot:

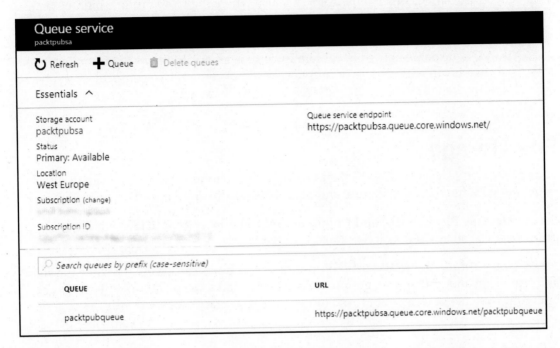

Figure 2.14: The created queue

 For developers who are interested in learning how to access a created Queue and start working with it, you can check the following link: `https://docs.microsoft.com/en-us/azure/storage/storage-dotnet-how-to-use-queues`.

Queue storage key points

The following tips should be considered, as they will help you when designing your storage solution using the Queues service:

- Queue messages can be up to 64 KB in size, however, a Queue can contain messages up to the limiting size of the storage account.
- The maximum lifetime of a message in a queue is 7 days.

- As mentioned previously, messages follow the FIFO order, however, they can be out of order if an application crash occurs, which is why it would be better to use Azure Service Bus queues for a scenario where the FIFO order is highly important.
- Messages can be scheduled for delivery later.
- A Queue name may only contain lowercase letters, hyphens, and numbers, and must begin with a letter or number. It cannot contain two consecutive hyphens. Name length varies from between 3 and 63 characters.

File storage

The File storage service is the easiest and coolest service to work with. You can use it to create network file shares on Azure, and access them from anywhere in the world.

Server Message Block (**SMB**) and **Common Internet File System** (**CIFS**) are the only protocols that can be used to access these file shares.

As a result, multiple Azure VMs and on-premises machines can access the same file share and have read and write privileges on it. Azure File shares can be mounted to different operating systems, such as, Windows, Linux, and even macOS concurrently.

File storage advantages

The File storage service has some good reasons to use it, which are:

- **Software as a service (SaaS) service**: The Azure File storage service is considered a SaaS service because you do not have to manage the hardware, operating system, patches, and so on. It is simply fully managed.
- **Shareability**: It can be shared across multiple machines providing read and write privileges for all of those machines.
- **Automation**: It supports working with PowerShell and the Azure CLI, which can be used to create scripts to automate repetitive tasks with minimal administration.
- **Flexibility and high availability**: Using the Azure File storage service eliminates concerns regarding administration and outage issues that you face with traditional file servers.

Creating File storage

Let's see how we can create File storage in the storage account we created in the last chapter.

1. Navigate to the storage we created in the last chapter using the portal, as shown in the following screenshot:

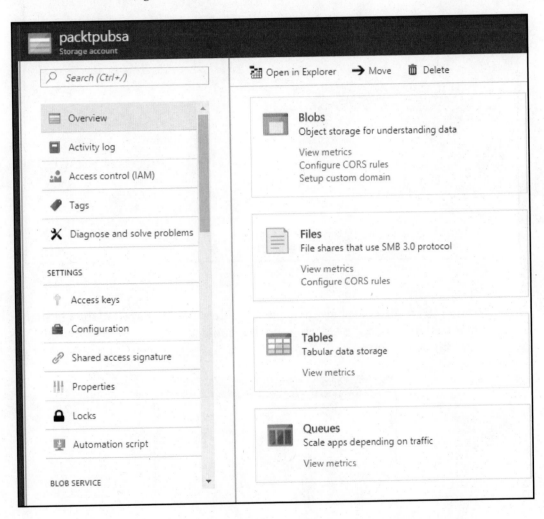

Figure 2.15: Azure Storage services

2. You can see all the storage services in the previous screenshot. To manage files, you have to click on **Files** and a new blade will appear, as shown in the following screenshot:

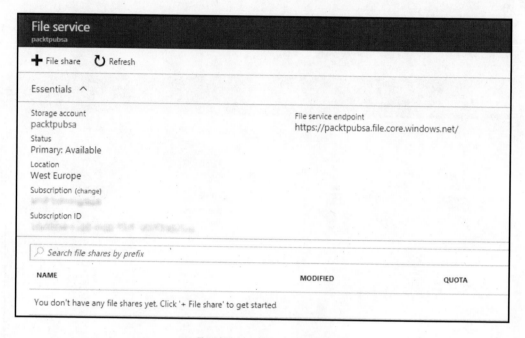

Figure 2.16: Azure File service overview

3. In order to create a file share, just click on **File share**, and specify the file share **Name** and its **Quota**, considering that the quota is optional, as shown in the following screenshot:

Figure 2.17: Azure File share creation

4. Once done, you will see that the file share has been created, as shown in the following screenshot. Considering that we never specified a quota, it used the maximum space the storage account can store; therefore, you have to design your file share properly according to your needs, and with the proper quota, to avoid any future issues caused by the space used. Also, you can change the quota even after file share creation:

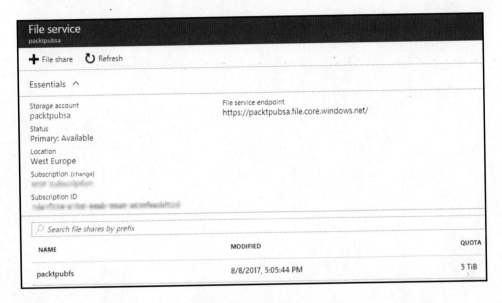

Figure 2.18: The created file share

5. You can map the file share to your Windows machine or Linux machine, adding directories within the file share, uploading data to it, and so on, if you opened it after creation, as shown in the following screenshot:

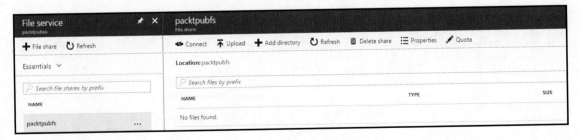

Figure 2.19: Overview of the created file share

6. To map the file share as a drive on your Windows machine or Linux machine, click on **Connect**, which will open a new blade, displaying the commands required to map it to your machine, as shown in the following screenshot:

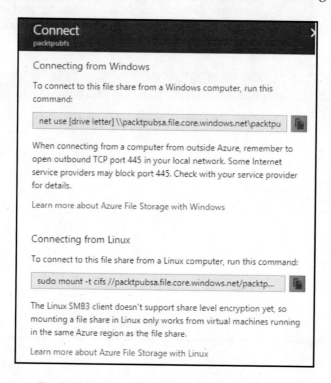

Figure 2.20: Connecting to your file share from your Windows or Linux Machine

7. To upload files to it, click on **Upload** and browse for the desired file, as shown in the following screenshot:

Figure 2.21: Uploading a file to the file share

File storage key points

The following tips should be considered, as they will help you when designing your storage solution using the File service:

- Since SMB 2.1 does not support encryption, then only the VMs within the same region as the storage account will be able to access it if you are using SMB 2.1. As a result, you have to consider that you cannot access the read-only data available in another region if you are using **Read-access geo-redundant storage (RA-GRS)** as a replication type.
- Since SMB 3.0 S supports encryption, you will be able to mount the file share to any VM around the globe, but port 445 must be opened.
- At the time of writing, only 2 versions of macOS were supported for Azure File shares (Sierra 10.12, and El Capitan 10.11).
- For better performance when working with Azure File shares on macOS, I recommend disabling SMB packet signing.
- The maximum size of a file share is 5 TB, considering that a file in the file share cannot exceed 1 TB.
- Every Azure File share supports up to 1000 IOPS, and 60 MB/s throughput.
- File share names can contain only lowercase letters, numbers, and hyphens, and must begin and end with a letter or number. The name cannot contain two consecutive hyphens.

 At the time of writing, Active Directory-based authentication and **Access Control Lists (ACLs)** are not supported. However, you can assign specific users to access specific file shares, but unfortunately, you cannot customize them anymore because every user has permission to a specific file share, which will be full access to the share.

Understanding the Azure Storage architecture

Learning how to work with Azure Storage and how to design it to fit your solution is everyone's purpose, but learning what is going on behind the scenes and what every piece means is what makes you an expert.

Azure Storage is a distributed storage software stack built by Microsoft. The storage access architecture consists of the following three layers:

- Front-End layer
- Partition layer
- Stream layer

Front-End layer

The Front-End layer is responsible for receiving incoming requests, their authentication, and authorization, and then delivers them to a partition server in the Partition layer.

You may wonder, how does the frontend know which partition server to forward each request to? The answer is pretty easy, because the frontend caches a partition map.

And here, a new question will pop up, what is a partition map? It is responsible for keeping track of the partitions of the storage service being accessed, and which partition server controls access to each partition in the system.

Partition layer

The Partition layer is responsible for partitioning all the data objects in the system. Not only that, it is also responsible for assigning the partitions to partition servers, plus load balancing the partitions across partition servers to meet the traffic needs of the storage services, considering that a single partition server would handle multiple partitions.

Stream layer

The Stream layer or **Distributed and replicated File System (DFS)** layer is the layer responsible for storing bits on the disk and the data durability as it distributes and replicates data across many servers. All data stored in this layer is accessible from any partition server.

Sparse storage and TRIM in Azure

When you create a VHD on Azure to store your data on it, all the space you have chosen as a size for your VHD is completely allocated because Azure uses fixed-size VHDs. Therefore, you may wonder, will I really pay for the whole space even if I'm not using it, especially as it is not a dynamic disk but a fixed one.

Let's discuss this in more detail.

When you create a VHD, all the size is allocated, and that might trick you into using smaller VHDs to save costs, but actually that is not what really happens behind the scenes.

Azure uses sparse storage, which means no matter the size of the VHD you have created, you will only pay for what you have stored on the VHD. For example, you have a 1 TB VHD, but you have only 200 MB of storage stored on it. You will only pay for the 200 MB storage, therefore as a best practice, you should create the VHD with the maximum storage to avoid any downtime later during the resizing process.

Microsoft does its best to charge you only for what you use, that's why Azure Storage supports TRIM, which means whenever you delete data from it, you no longer pay for the deleted storage.

 When you add a VHD, you should use quick format for the disk, not the full format. Doing so will write OS to the entire disk, which means you will have to pay for the entire disk. You should also consider not using defragmentation to avoid the movement of the disk blocks, which means greater costs will have to be paid. For further information about the Azure Storage architecture, you can download the following PDF file: http://www.sigops.org/sosp/sosp11/current/2011-Cascais/11-calder-online.pdf.

Securing Azure Storage

It's great to know how to manage Azure Storage, and even to follow best practices throughout the process. However, securing your storage should be your biggest concern, especially because storage is the base on which all your **Infrastructure as a service (IaaS)** services run.

Throughout this topic, we will cover the following methods to secure Azure Storage:

- **Role-Based Access Control (RBAC)**
- Access keys
- **Shared access signature (SAS)**

RBAC

Giving every user the exact permissions they need should be your first concern in order to avoid a complete disaster if a user's credentials were exposed.

RBAC would help you with segregating duties within your team; specifically, everyone would only be granted the required permissions to get their job done.

RBAC role assignments would be granted based on:

- Subscription
- Resource group
- Resource

For example, RBAC can be used to grant permissions for a user to manage the virtual machines within a subscription, or to grant permissions for a user to manage a complete resource group that contains virtual machines, **network interfaces** (**NICs**), storage accounts, availability sets, and so on, or granting permissions for a user to manage a specific resource such as a specific virtual machine. This does not deny the fact that the same user can be granted permissions to another resource, resource group, or even a subscription.

Granting the reader role to a user using RBAC

Throughout this topic, we will cover how to grant a user read permissions on our previously created storage account, `packtpubsa`. So, without further ado, let's get started.

1. First, you must have a user in the Azure Active Directory. If not, you can learn how via the following link: `https://docs.microsoft.com/en-us/azure/active-directory/active-directory-users-create-azure-portal`.

2. Open the Azure portal and navigate to **Storage account**, then select the storage account you want the user to have read permissions on, as shown in the following screenshot:

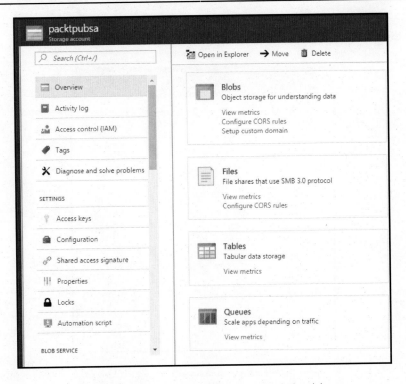

Figure 2.22: Azure Storage account on which we will grant a user read permissions

3. Navigate to **Access control (IAM)** and click on **Add**, as shown in the following screenshot:

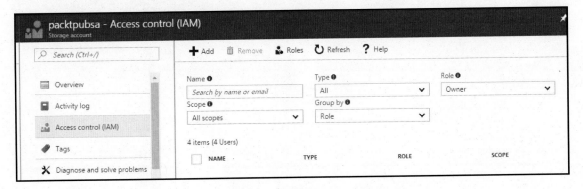

Figure 2.23: Access control blade

4. Select the **Role**, which in our case is **Reader** role, and select the user you are willing to grant this role to, as shown in the following screenshot:

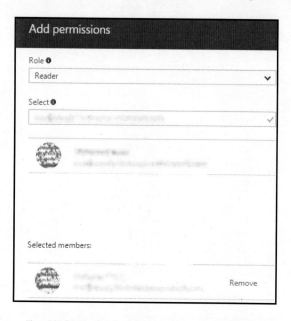

Figure 2.24: Selecting the role and the user to which the role is being granted

5. Once done, you will see it under **READER** role in **Access control (IAM)** blade, as shown in the following screenshot:

Figure 2.25: The users with reader role access to packtpubsa storage account

To learn more about RBAC, you can check out the following links:

- RBAC built-in roles: `https://docs.microsoft.com/en-us/azure/active-directory/role-based-access-built-in-roles`
- Custom roles in Azure RBAC: `https://docs.microsoft.com/en-us/azure/active-directory/role-based-access-control-custom-roles`.

Access keys

Storage account access keys are 512-bit strings, which are generated once you create a new storage account, and get paired with it. These keys are for authenticating storage services whenever you try to access them.

Fortunately, Azure provides two access keys. So, if the primary key is compromised, you can regenerate the key, and use the secondary key in the meantime.

To regenerate access keys, you have to navigate to the storage account, then navigate to **Access keys** under **SETTINGS**, as shown in the following screenshot:

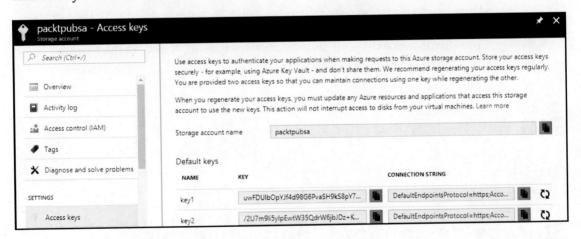

Figure 2.26: Storage account access keys

To regenerate the keys, you have to click on the regenerate icon, as shown in the following screenshot:

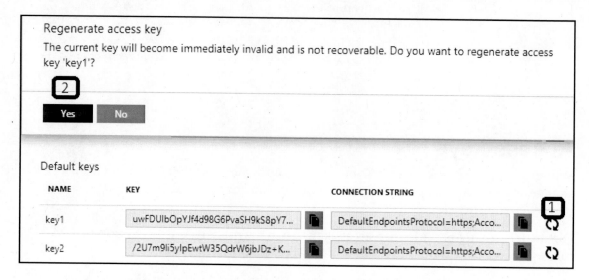

Figure 2.27: Regenerating the primary key

 Whenever you regenerate the access key, you have to update all the clients who were using the old access key to access the storage account to avoid any disruption with your storage services that are based on the storage account for which the access keys were changed.

SAS

SAS will be covered in `Chapter 8`, *Extending Your Azure Storage Management* in the *Azure Storage Explorer* section.

Storage design for highly available applications

What we have covered so far shows the importance of Azure Storage as a cornerstone for building whatever you want to build on Azure. Therefore, in this topic, we will cover some of the most important features you have to implement in order to be able to design highly available storage for your applications.

The following points should be our main focus when designing a highly available storage solution:

- RA-GRS
- Azure Backup
- Azure Site Recovery
- Premium Storage

RA-GRS

RA-GRS is the highest durable replication type, as was covered in the last chapter. Not only this, but it also gives you read access to your storage in another region, which may reduce latency if you have to query your storage from a place that is nearer to the that region than the primary region, considering that you will access the **Last Sync Time** value, as Azure uses asynchronous replication between regions.

But, you might wonder, what if the primary region was completely destroyed, and your application needed to make write operations to the storage? The answer is simple, Microsoft will failover the other region, but not immediately, it might take some time. Therefore, for a complete guide about what to do if a storage outage occurs, how to prepare for it, and even how to detect it, you can check out the following link: `https://docs.` `microsoft.com/en-us/azure/storage/storage-disaster-recovery-guidance`.

> At the time of writing, all storage services can be queried in the secondary regions when using RA-GRS except file services.

Azure Backup

Lately, many enterprises have been exposed to piracy, especially ransomware. Without having a backup of your storage, your data might be encrypted, and you will have to either pay to get it decrypted, or you will never see it again. That is why considering Azure Backup as a part of you design will be very beneficial to keeping your application highly available.

Further details about Azure Backup will be covered in `Chapter 8`, *Extending Your Azure Storage Management*.

Azure Site Recovery

If you have your application built on Azure VMs, or even on-premises VMs, you have to make sure that there's a disaster recovery site for your environment, and to do so you can user Azure Site Recovery.

Azure Site Recovery will replicate changes to the VMs' virtual hard disks, so, whatever happens, you will be good to go with your disaster recovery site, keeping your application highly available.

Further details about Azure Site Recovery will be covered in Chapter 8, *Extending Your Azure Storage Management*.

Premium Storage

Using Premium Storage will increase the performance of your application; as a result, it will be highly available. Azure Premium Storage has a throughput rate of up to 50 GBps and 80,000 IOPs. Using storage with such specifications can make not only a highly available application, but also an application with super-fast performance.

Understanding client libraries

When we created our storage account, the name of the account took the following format `storageaccount.core.windows.net`.

So, it is no surprise that all the storage service's endpoints took the following format:

- **Blob**: `storageaccount.blob.core.windows.net`
- **Table**: `storageaccount.table.core.windows.net`
- **Queue**: `storageaccount.queue.core.windows.net`
- **File**: `storageaccount.file.core.windows.net`

These endpoints are exposed through REST APIs to be accessed by any platform using HTTP.

That is why Microsoft provides several client libraries to give developers a high level of control over Azure Storage services.

Azure Storage supports many client libraries for many platforms, such as:

- .NET
- Java
- Node.js
- PHP
- Ruby
- Python
- C++
- iOS
- Android

Microsoft keeps adding new client libraries, so don't be surprised if you find that new client libraries have been added when you are reading this book. That is what Microsoft does with its cloud services, it keeps adding new features, and supports new things.

> For further information about how to use client libraries, you can check out the following links:
>
> - .NET: `https://docs.microsoft.com/en-us/dotnet/api/overview/azure/storage?view=azure-dotnet`
> - Java: `https://docs.microsoft.com/en-us/java/api/overview/azure/storage`
> - Node.js: `http://azure.github.io/azure-storage-node/`
> - PHP: `http://azure.github.io/azure-storage-php/`
> - Ruby: `http://azure.github.io/azure-storage-ruby/`
> - Python: `https://azure-storage.readthedocs.io/en/latest/index.html`
> - C++: `http://azure.github.io/azure-storage-cpp/`
> - iOS: `https://github.com/Azure/azure-storage-ios`
> - Android: `http://azure.github.io/azure-storage-android/`

Automating tasks

As usual when we reach the end of a chapter, we will work on automating the tasks that we have done manually. So, let's get started.

Creating Blob storage using PowerShell

In this topic, we will cover how to create Blob storage that everyone has read/write access to in the storage account we created in the last chapter:

```
$ContainerName = packtpubbs

$SAK = Get-AzureRmStorageAccountKey -StorageAccountName "packtpubsaps" -
ResourceGroupName packtpub

$SAK = $SAK | Where {$_.KeyName -like "key1"}

$SC = New-AzureStorageContext -StorageAccountName packtpubsaps -
StorageAccountKey $SAK.Value

New-AzureStorageContainer -Name $ContainerName -Permission Container -
Context $SC

Set-AzureStorageBlobContent -Container $ContainerName -File C:\test.txt -
Context $SC
```

Steps in detail:

1. Create a variable for the container name, so you do not have to write it repeatedly.
2. Create a variable for the storage account key named `$SAK`, within which the access keys will be stored.
3. Since you need the primary key only, you have to select it and put it into the same variable.
4. Then, you have to create a storage context which encapsulates the storage account credentials, named `$SC`.
5. As the blob needs a container to be created within, you have to create a new one, considering that the `Permission` parameter refers to **Access type** in the portal, in addition to specifying the `Context` to know in which storage account this container will be created.
6. Once done, you can start to upload your storage to the blob.

In the beginning, we have got to create a storage account key variable, `$SAK`, within which there will be the access key values. But, since we only need the primary key, we have got to select that key and put it into the `$SAK` variable.

The private access type in PowerShell is changed to Off, so consider that when you want to create a container with the private access type using PowerShell.

Creating Blob storage using the Azure CLI 2.0

Let's repeat the previous task, but this time, we are going to use the Azure CLI 2.0:

```
az storage container create --name packtpubbs --public-access container --
account-name packtpubsacli

az storage blob upload --file C:\test.txt --container-name packtpubbs --
name blobcli --account-name packtpubsacli
```

In the preceding command, we have only changed the storage account, which we have created to be used in tasks implemented by the Azure CLI 2.0, and we named the blob blobcli.

 The private access type in the Azure CLI is changed to Off, so consider that when you want to create a container with the private access type using the Azure CLI.

Creating Table storage using PowerShell

Using the same session opened in PowerShell in the previous task, let's create a table.

```
New-AzureStorageTable -Name packtpubtable -Context $SC
```

Creating Table storage using the Azure CLI 2.0

Creating a table using the Azure CLI 2.0 is very straightforward; you only have to specify the name of the table and the storage account within which the table will be created:

```
az storage table create --name packtpubtable --account-name packtpubsacli
```

Creating Queue storage using PowerShell

Using the same PowerShell session, let's create a queue:

```
New-AzureStorageQueue -Name packtpubqueue -Context $SC
```

Creating Queue storage using the Azure CLI 2.0

Again, we will just follow the same format as the storage services we created previously:

```
az storage queue create --name packtpubqueue --account-name packtpubsacli
```

Creating a file share using PowerShell

At the moment, there are no cmdlets available to create file shares on Azure, but they are expected to be available soon.

Granting the reader role to a user with RBAC using PowerShell

Let's grant a user the reader role using RBAC via PowerShell to a resource group:

```
New-AzureRmRoleAssignment -ResourceGroupName PacktPub -SignInName
x@company.com -RoleDefinitionName Reader
```

Considering that the SignInName parameter is the SignInName of the user you want to assign read access to.

Granting the reader role for a user with RBAC using the Azure CLI 2.0

There is no big difference between the parameters used in this example, compared to the ones used in PowerShell.

```
az role assignment create --assignee x@company.com --role Reader --
resource-group PacktPub
```

Regenerating storage account access keys using PowerShell

In creating Blob storage using PowerShell, you learned how to retrieve storage account access keys. Using the same PowerShell session, we will regenerate the keys.

```
New-AzureRmStorageAccountKey -StorageAccountName packtpubsaps -KeyName key1
-ResourceGroupName PacktPub
```

Considering that `key1` is the primary key and `key2` is the secondary key.

Regenerating storage account access keys using the Azure CLI 2.0

At the moment, there are no commands to regenerate storage account access keys using the Azure CLI 2.0, however, they are expected to be available soon.

Summary

So far, we have gone through Azure Storage in detail, illustrating Azure Storage services, its architecture, and even how to secure it. Then, we proposed some storage design best practices to keep your application highly available, and since Azure Storage is not only managed through the portal, Azure PowerShell, and Azure CLI, we briefly talked about the client libraries that are most suitable for developers. At the end of the chapter, we automated the tasks that have been implemented so far.

Next, Azure Virtual Machines and their dependency on Azure Storage will be covered in detail. Therefore, the knowledge gained in this chapter is required for a better understanding of the coming chapter.

3
Azure Storage for VMs

In this chapter, we will go through the relationship between Azure **Virtual Machines** (**VMs**) and Azure Storage. The chapter will kick off by introducing Azure VMs, moving forward to how to create these VMs, then you will learn about the storage considerations you need to take care of to get a better design for your environment, and even how to capture images from these VMs. Finally, you will learn how to automate these tasks.

The following topics will be covered:

- An introduction to Azure VMs
- Creating an Azure VM
- Storage considerations for Azure VMs
- Capturing VMs
- Automating your common tasks with Azure VM storage

An introduction to Azure VMs

Azure VMs is the most well-known, usable, and oldest service available in Azure. Azure VMs provides the deployment of different flavors of Windows and Linux VMs.

Using Azure VMs provides you with full control over the configuration and management of a VM. Management refers to installing software, patching, and even maintaining a VM.

It is no surprise that, when you create a normal VM, whether it is on-premises or off-premises, you need storage for the VM's virtual hard disk. That leads us to understanding that Azure VMs use Azure Storage as a storage provider, and that is what I am going to cover in detail throughout this chapter.

But before getting started and getting our hands dirty with playing with Azure VMs, I'm going to illustrate some confusing points regarding them.

Fortunately, Microsoft bills VMs per minute, not per hour, therefore, when you use a VM for 30 minutes, you will only be charged for 30 minutes. Also, when a VM is not running, you will not be charged for the computing resources (CPU and Memory), however, you will be charged for the VM storage, so let's discuss VM states in more detail:

State	Description
Running	The VM is running and you get charged for usage as usual
Stopped	The VM is shut down by Windows/Linux, but you still get charged for the VM, as it still deployed to the same physical host and resources are still reserved for it
Stopped (deallocated)	The VM is stopped by the stop button on the VM blade via the Azure portal

At the time of writing, Microsoft has two **Service Level Agreements (SLAs)** for Azure VMs:

- Two or more VMs within the same availability set have 99.95% availability to one VM guaranteed
- Using a single VM that uses Premium Storage will provide at least 99.9% availability

 To keep updated on Microsoft SLAs for Azure VMs, keep your eye on the following link: `https://azure.microsoft.com/en-us/support/legal/sla/virtual-machines/v1_6/`.

Azure VMs series

Azure VMs have multiple series to fit different cases and scenarios:

- **A Series**: This series is most commonly used in development and test scenarios
- **D Series**: This series has a fast CPU and **solid-state drives (SSD)** disks, and is most commonly used for general-purpose computing, such as relational databases, and every application that requires high IOPs
- **F Series**: This series targets applications that require intensive compute power, such as web servers

- **G Series**: This series targets applications that require high memory and fast storage, such as ERP, and SAP solutions
- **H Series**: This series has very high compute capabilities, and might fit in scenarios that require high performance, such as analytics
- **L Series**: This series is dedicated to applications that require low latency, high throughput, high IOPs, and large size disks, such as NoSQL databases
- **N Series**: This series has high GPU capabilities, and fits scenarios such as video editing, graphics rendering, and so on

 For further information about Azure VMs series and the new series that will be added, you can check the following link: `https://azure.microsoft.com/en-us/pricing/details/virtual-machines/series/`.

Creating an Azure VM

Before diving further into Azure VMs and their concerns with Azure Storage, let's create an Azure VM:

1. Open the Azure portal and navigate to **Virtual machines**, as shown in the following screenshot:

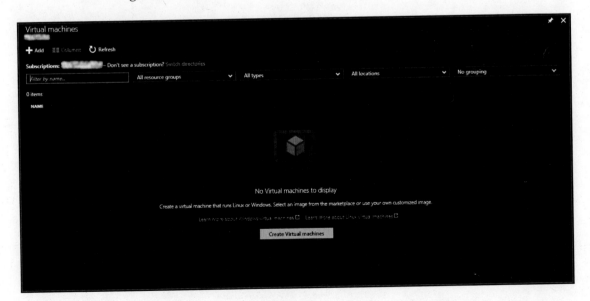

Figure 3.1: Azure VMs blade overview

2. Click on **Create Virtual Machines** to select an OS image for the VM.
3. For the sake of this demonstration, I'll select **Windows Server 2016 Datacenter**, as shown in the following screenshot:

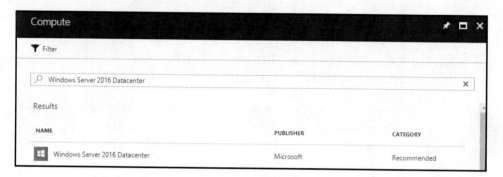

Figure 3.2: Selecting the image that is going to be used on the VM

4. Once you click on the image, you will be asked to determine the deployment model, as shown in the following screenshot:

Figure 3.3: Selecting the VM deployment model

5. Once you specify the deployment model, a new blade will pop up, and you will be asked to fill in the fields, as shown in the following screenshot:

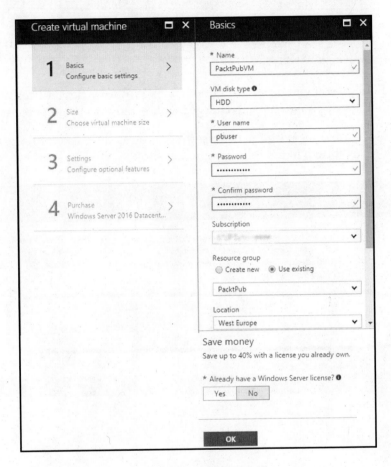

Figure 3.4: Filling in Azure VM basic info

Where:

- **Name**: The VM name
- **VM disk type**: There are two types of disks, HHD and SSD, and you can select the type according to your needs
- **Username and password**: The credentials that will be used to access the VM
- **Subscription**: If you have multiple subscriptions, you can select the desired subscription on which the VM will be billed

- **Resource group**: You have two options--to create a new one or select an existing group--and since a resource group was created in Chapter 1, *Understanding Azure Storage 101*, it will be used in this demonstration
- **Location**: Select the nearest region to you, so you can reduce latency

Finally, you will be asked if you have a Windows Server license or not, because if you do have it, charges will be reduced by 40 percent.

6. Once you are done with the basic settings, you will be asked to specify the size of the VM, as shown in the following screenshot:

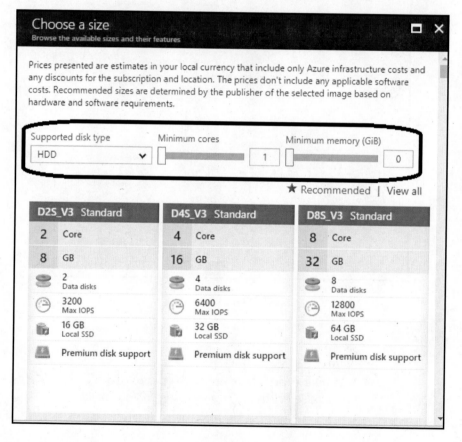

Figure 3.5: Selecting the VM size

Consider that you can shortlist the result of the size by determining the disk type, minimum cores, and minimum memory.

7. Once you select the size, the **Settings** blade will pop up, as shown in the following screenshot. Consider that none of the settings will be changed here, as I'll cover this in detail shortly:

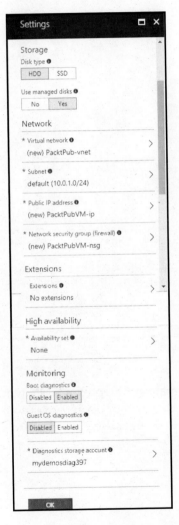

Figure 3.6: Azure VM settings

8. Once your settings are configured, you can go ahead and purchase the VM or you can download the template for the VM configuration that has been done so far and reuse it later to automate the process, as shown in the following screenshot:

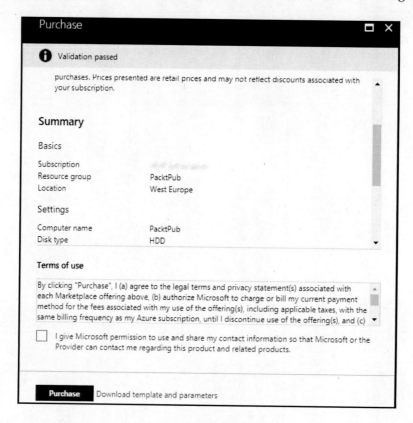

Figure 3.7: Purchasing the VM

 To learn how to create and deploy a JSON template, you can check the following URL https://docs.microsoft.com/en-us/azure/azure-resource-manager/resource-manager-create-first-template.

9. Once the VM is deployed, you can navigate to it, as shown in the following screenshot:

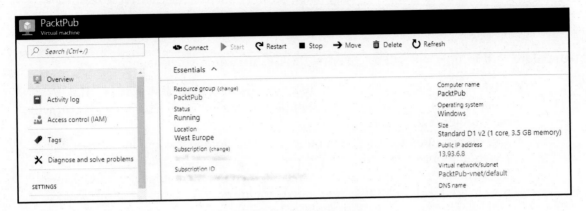

Figure 3.8: Overview of Azure VM

10. You can connect to the VM by clicking on **Connect**, which will download a preconfigured RDP file, and once you open it, you will be asked to enter the VM credentials, as shown in the following screenshot:

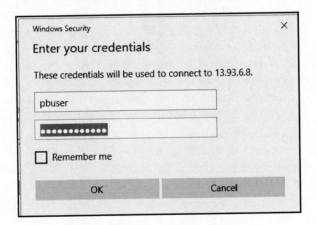

Figure 3.9: Connecting to the VM via RDP

To create a Linux VM, you have to go through the same steps that have been done so far; there aren't too many differences.

VM settings

During VM creation, you have to specify some settings, such as the disk type, the disk's manageability, some virtual network configuration, extensions, availability sets, and monitoring.

Therefore, in this topic, we will be covering these settings in further details:

- **Disk type**: Selecting the type of disk, whether it is **hard disk drives** (**HDD**), which means you will be using Standard Storage or SSD, which means you will be using Premium Storage.

- **Use managed disks**: Since you might create a storage account and forget that it has limitations in its IOPs, throughput, and so on. That could cause too many issues in the performance of the VMs assigned to that storage account because they exceed its limitations. But when using managed storage accounts, Microsoft will handle that for you. You will not be responsible for monitoring whether the storage account has exceeded its limitations or not, which would require a tedious calculation process for every service you are using that uses this storage account. Further details about managed and unmanaged disks will be covered in more detail shortly.

- **Virtual network**: It is common that, when you create a VM, you have to specify a virtual network for it, from which it will take an IP address that will allow the VM to communicate with another VM, and even to be communicated to:

    - **Subnet**: Is a part of the virtual network, as you can create multiple subnets within the same virtual network. For example, you might create a subnet for web servers and another one for database servers, however, they can communicate normally without the need to do some routing since they are in the same virtual network.

    - **Public IP address:** Since this VM is built on Azure, you cannot connect to it with its private IP address, as you will connect to it over the internet. That is why a public IP address has to be specified.

    - **Network security group:** This is considered the firewall for the whole virtual network, from which you can specify who can access the VMs and on which port, and can even control outbound traffic, specifying which VM can access the outside world and from which port.

- **Extensions**: As mentioned in the terminologies table in Chapter 1, *Understanding Azure Storage 101*, extensions are software components that extend VM functionality and simplify various management operations, such as adding an anti-malware solution to the VM during its deployment to be used later when you start managing the VM.
- **Availability set**: As mentioned in the terminologies table in Chapter 1, *Understanding Azure Storage 101*, availability set means that the VMs are spread over different fault domains and update domains, which ensures that, in the event of a rack failure, not all instances are brought down at the same time. If any updates are applied to a host on which there is one of your VMs and requires a restart, it will not be applied to the other VM within the same availability set.
- **Monitoring**: Where you will have to determine whether you want to monitor the VM booting and its OS or not:
    - **Boot diagnostics**: Your VM might get stuck while booting, especially if you are using your own image. In this case, boot diagnostics will be a huge benefit, as it will help you to diagnose and recover your VMs from failures.
    - **Guest OS diagnostics**: Will capture data from the running OS and the applications running on it, so you can diagnose your issues and recover from it.
    - **Diagnostics storage account**: Since the logs need a storage account to be stored in, you can create a dedicated account for diagnostics or even use an existing account. Considering that, I highly recommend using a dedicated storage account.

So far, I have covered the settings in a nutshell, however, there is more to be covered, but since that is beyond the scope of this book, it will not be covered here. However, you can check out the following links for further information about settings:

- Azure Virtual Networks: https://docs.microsoft.com/en-us/azure/virtual-network/virtual-networks-overview
- VM extensions: https://docs.microsoft.com/en-us/azure/virtual-machines/windows/extensions-features
- Availability sets: https://docs.microsoft.com/en-us/azure/virtual-machines/windows/manage-availability
- Monitoring: https://docs.microsoft.com/en-us/azure/monitoring-and-diagnostics/monitoring-overview-of-diagnostic-logs

Storage considerations for Azure VMs

As mentioned earlier, Azure VMs depend on Azure Storage to function properly. Therefore, let's go through some storage considerations for Azure VMs for a better design for your environment.

Managed versus unmanaged disks

As mentioned earlier, managed disks save lots of effort and even support Premium Storage and Standard Storage.

Managed disks key points

Let's cover some of the managed disks key points that may influence your design and even your decision when it comes to selecting whether to use managed disks or not:

- **Simplicity**: Using managed disks will eliminate lots of concerns when it comes to storage design because you will not have to consider the limitations of the storage account, such as IOPs. For example, if you have multiple VMs running and their disks are assigned to the same storage account, you might face some performance issues because the VMs' disks have exceeded the IOPs limitations.
- **Managed disks limits**: Managed disks support up to 10,000 disks per subscription, which means a massive number of VMs can be created within the same subscription using managed disks.
- **Reliability**: Using managed disks ensure that the disks of VM in an availability set are completely isolated by assigning disks to different storage scale units, so whenever a failure occurs in one of the VM disks, other VM disks are working properly.
- **Azure Storage Replication Support**: At the moment, managed disks support only the **Locally Redundant Storage (LRS)** replication type.
- **Azure Backup support**: Managed disks support Azure Backup and it is a very important thing to consider because, if the data center in which your storage exists get damaged, you must have a backup of your storage in another region.

- **Snapshot support**: Managed disks support snapshot, which is a read-only copy of a managed disk, therefore, can be used as a backup method. Consider that snapshotted storage gets charged independently based on its size.

> A snapshot can only be taken from one disk at a time, so if you have multiple disks that use one of the RAID techniques, you cannot restore the disks again with the same state, because snapshots have no awareness of that.

- **Images support**: When you want to create an image from a Sysprepped VM, you can capture an image of all its managed disks so it can be used later as a template to create other VMs.

> Images and snapshots are completely different. An image is a like a VM template that can be used to recreate other VMs with the same specifications, and that includes the disks attached to it. However, snapshots are a point in time of one disk. For example, a snapshot of a disk can be considered as a backup for a disk until the moment the snapshot is taken and can be reused for other VMs later.

- When using Azure, you have to consider that everything comes with a price. Most of the time, it is not expensive; however, when using managed disks, you must consider storage type, disk size, and so on, because that adds more credits.

> To calculate the expected credits for using managed disks according to your environment size, please go to the pricing calculator via the following link: `https://azure.microsoft.com/en-us/pricing/calculator/`, and for further information about pricing and billing for Azure managed disks, you can check the following link: `https://docs.microsoft.com/en-us/azure/storage/storage-managed-disks-overview#pricing-and-billing`.

VM disks

Whenever you create a VM, there will be only one disk attached to it, but there are some other disks that can be added to Azure VMs, so let's figure out the types of VM disks:

- **OS disk**: The disk on which the operating system files exist, which is the C drive by default for Windows, and dev/sda for Linux. The OS disk size can be up to 2 TB.

- **Temporary disk**: This disk exists by default in any VM, but as its name suggests, it is temporary, which means it is non-persistent. In other words, whenever your VM is turned off, the data will be lost. This disk provides temporary storage and uses the drive letter D by default in Windows, and /dev/sdb1 in Linux. Temporary storage exists in the physical host of the VM, but since the VM could be moved to any other host at any time due to a failure in that physical host, your data will be lost. Also, the temporary disk size varies based on the VM size. In addition to this, when using temporary storage, you will not incur any charges. If you restart the VM via Windows, you will not lose the data that exists in the temporary storage disk; otherwise, you will lose it if any downtime occurs for whatever reason.

One of the most common uses for the temporary disk is storing paging files. After all, every time the VM starts up, the paging file will be created in the temporary storage.

- **Data disk**: This disk is not added to the VM by default, you will have to add it yourself, as you will see shortly. Data disks are used to store permanent data, which means it is persistent. For example, you can save your SQL database or any other application data. At the moment, the data disk maximum size is almost 4 TB, but you can add more than one data disk to a VM, depending on the VM size.

All disks can use the Standard or Premium Storage, based on your selection of the storage type and the VM size.

Microsoft has made a good comparison of Azure Premium Disks versus Azure Standard Disks, as shown in the following table:

	Azure Premium Disk	Azure Standard Disk
Disk Type	Solid State Drives (SSD)	Hard Disk Drives (HDD)
Overview	SSD-based high-performance, low-latency disk support for VMs running IO-intensive workloads or hosting mission critical production environment	HDD-based cost effective disk support for Dev/Test VM scenarios
Scenario	Production and performance sensitive workloads	Dev/Test, non-critical, Infrequent access
Disk Size	P4: 32 GB (Managed Disks only) P6: 64 GB (Managed Disks only) P10: 128 GB P20: 512 GB P30: 1024 GB P40: 2048 GB P50: 4095 GB	Unmanaged Disks: 1 GB – 4 TB (4095 GB) Managed Disks: S4: 32 GB S6: 64 GB S10: 128 GB S20: 512 GB S30: 1024 GB S40: 2048 GB S50: 4095 GB
Max Throughput per Disk	250 MB/s	60 MB/s
Max IOPS per Disk	7500 IOPS	500 IOPS

Reference: `https://docs.microsoft.com/en-us/azure/storage/storage-about-disks-and-vhds-windows#types-of-disks.`

Adding a data disk to Azure VM

Nothing is better than getting our hands dirty after understanding what is going on, so without further ado, let's get started:

1. Navigate to the VM we created earlier, as shown in the following screenshot:

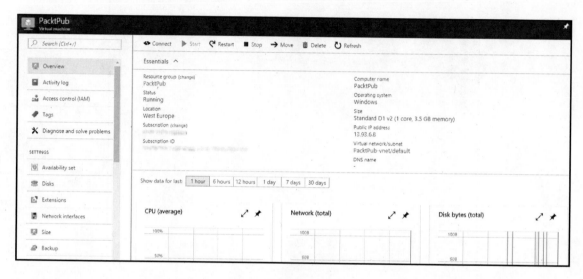

Figure 3.10: Overview of Azure VM

2. Navigate to **Disks**, which exists under **SETTINGS**, as shown in the following screenshot:

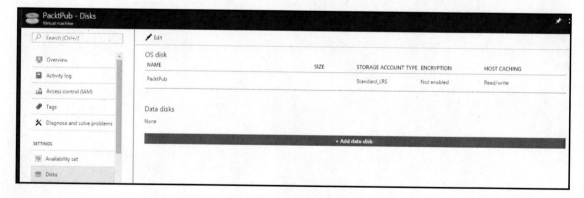

Figure 3.11: Azure VM disk overview

3. You will notice that only OS disk is added, and here you may wonder, where is the temporary disk? The answer is it is not here because, as I mentioned earlier, it is a part of the VM physical host, but in order to see it, you must open the VM, and navigate to **This PC**, as shown in the following screenshot:

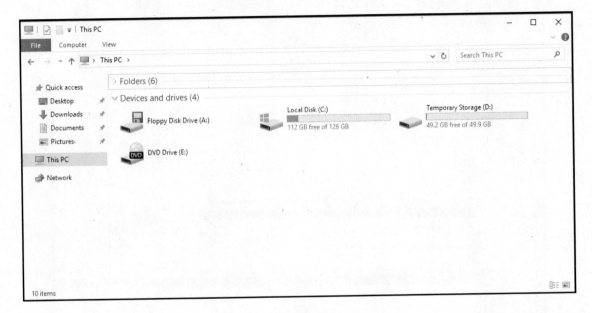

Figure 3.12: VM disks

4. Let's get back to our main purpose, which is adding a data disk. You have to click on **Add data disks** and fill in the fields, as shown in the following screenshot:

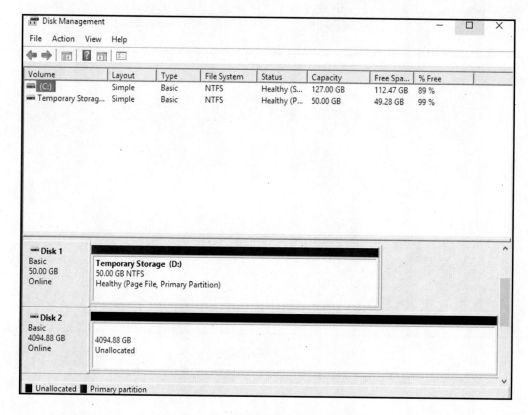

Figure 3.13: Adding a data disk

Where:

- **Name**: The name of the disk
- **Source type**: Selecting whether it is a new disk to be added or you are adding an existing disk from an existing blob
- **Account type**: Whether it is Standard or Premium
- **Size**: I entered the maximum size, as Microsoft supports sparse and trimming
- **Storage container**: Browse for the container on which you are willing to put that disk
- **Storage blob name**: The name of the blob on which the disk is stored

5. Once you click on **OK**, you will be navigated back to the disks blade and you have to save what you have done, as shown in the following screenshot:

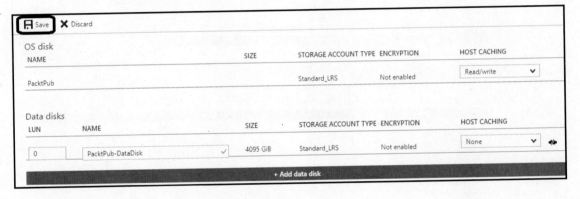

Figure 3.14: Saving the added data disk

6. Once you are done with adding the data disk, you have to open the **Disk Management** in the VM, as shown in the following screenshot:

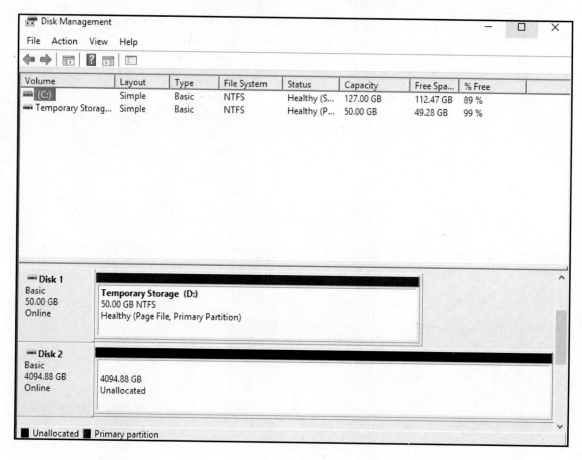

Figure 3.15: Initializing the new data disk

7. Hover over the unallocated space and start the creation of a new partition.
8. Once you are done, space will be allocated, and the data disk will be ready to use, as shown in the following screenshot:

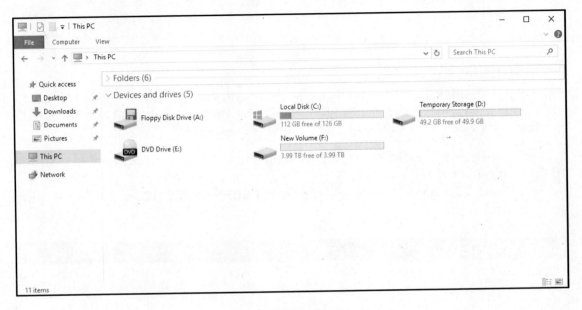

Figure 3.16: The new data disk

Data disks key points

For a better understanding about data disks, you have to take the following key points into consideration:

- Adding more data disks increases the IOPs, and throughput, especially if you are using stripping
- Do not use **Full Format** because that will fill the disk clusters with OS, which means the disk will appear to be filled with data, and as a result, you will have to pay for the whole disk, whether you use it partially, or completely

- Trimming is supported for at least Windows Server 2012/ Windows 8 for Windows-based VMs
- For further information about attaching disks to Linux VMs in Azure, check out the following link: `https://docs.microsoft.com/en-us/azure/virtual-machines/linux/tutorial-manage-disks#create-and-attach-disks`

Resizing disks

As I mentioned earlier, I recommend using the disks with their maximum size, however, if you already have some disks created and want to resize them, or even want to resize the OS disk (because by default it is 127 GB), you can follow these steps:

1. Navigate to the VM, stop it, and wait until its status turns to **Stopped (deallocated)**.
2. Navigate to **Disks**, which is located under **SETTINGS**, as shown in the following screenshot:

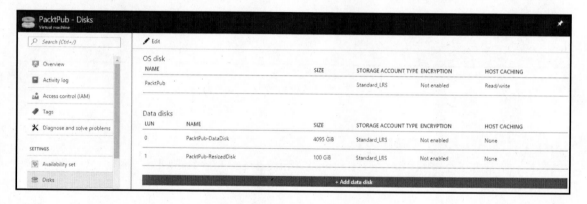

Figure 3.17: Azure VM disks

3. Navigate to the OS disk.

4. Enter the size you wish the disk to be, as shown in the following screenshot:

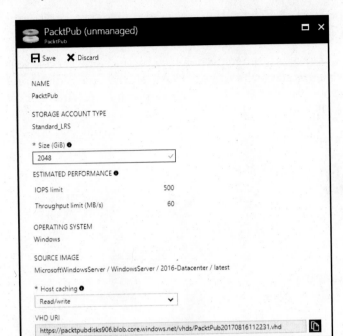

Figure 3.18: Resizing the OS disk

 At the time of writing, the maximum size for the OS disk is 2 TB. Also, size reduction is not supported; you can only expand the disk's size.

5. Once you are done, click on **Save**.

 It is a pretty straightforward process, but the main drawback is the downtime that must take place in order to resize the disks.

Host caching

I bet you noticed the **Host caching** option when adding and resizing Azure VM disks, and that is what we are going to cover in this topic.

As you know, the VM and its storage do not exist on the same server, so some latency occurs when a VM tries to access its storage that is stored on OS disks and data disks. Therefore, in order to reduce this latency, Microsoft came up with host caching, which caches access to the OS and data disks.

There are three types of host caching:

- Read-only
- Read/write
- None

Read-only

The read option writes through the cache.

Read/write

This is the default option for the OS disk, and it writes back to the cache.

None

In the none host caching mode, there will be no data caching. This is the default option for data disks.

Host caching key points

The following key points highlight some considerations for host caching:

- Use the none caching mode for disks on which logs are stored, because logs will do intensive write operations Also, there is no benefit to using the read-only mode for logs. Therefore, none is the best fit in such a situation.

- Use the read-only caching mode for disks on which the SQL data needs to be queried frequently from the SQL database because that will help to lower the latency and data retrieval.
- Do not use read/write just for any applications, because the data is cached in the VM memory, and whenever a crash happens to the VM, the data will be lost. So, you have to read more about the application you are hosting in your VM to know which type would be the best fit for it. For example, SQL server has the ability to handle writing cached data to persistent storage disks without the intervention of anything.
- The OS disk has two host caching options:
    - Read/Write: This is the default choice
    - Read Only
- The data disk has the three host caching options:
    - Read/Write
    - Read Only
    - None: This is the default
- The write cache is stored in memory in the host OS.
- The read cache is stored both on disk and in memory in the host OS.

Changing the host caching type

You might want to change the host caching type for disks according to your needs, so let's go through a step-by-step guide to get this implemented:

1. Navigate to the VM whose disks caching type you want to change.
2. Navigate to the **Disks** blade, which is located under **SETTINGS**.

3. Navigate to the disk whose caching type you want to change, as shown in the following screenshot:

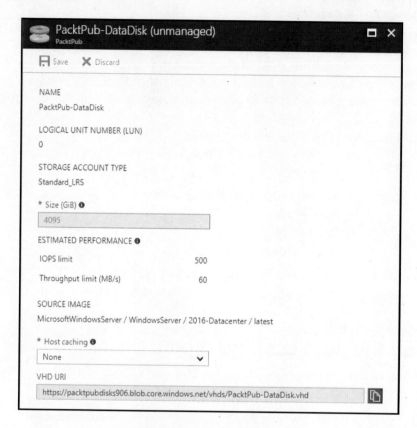

Figure 3.19: Azure VM Disk Properties

4. Under **Host caching**, select the type of caching you want. For example, **Read-only**, as shown in the following screenshot:

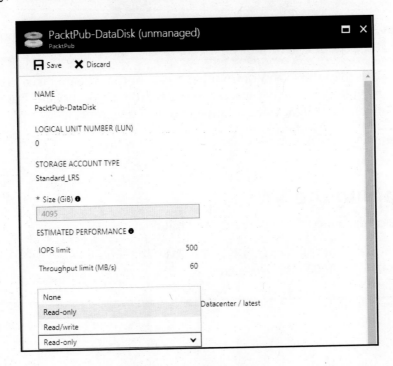

Figure 3.20: Changing the caching type

5. Once you are done, click on **Save**.

Changing the cache settings of an Azure disk detaches and reattaches the target disk. Therefore, consider stopping all applications and services that might be affected by changing this setting.

Capturing VMs

Templates … Templates … Templates…

That is what we always seek when we need to create a machine with the same specifications regularly, especially in dev/test environments.

So, what would you do if you wanted to have an image of a VM that you could use later to recreate other VMs without having to do all the steps you did to get this VM up and running?

The answer is very easy to say and easily implemented. You only need to capture the VM, considering that the image will include all the disks added to that VM.

There are two ways to capture the VM from the Azure portal. The first is, if you use managed storage, you will directly capture the image from the VM blade. But if you use unmanaged storage, you will navigate to **Images** and start capturing the VM.

But before doing any of that, you have to sysprep the VM first.

Sysprepping the VM

Before you proceed, connect to the VM first and follow these steps:

1. Navigate to the following path in the VM C:\Windows\System32\Sysprep, as shown in the following screenshot:

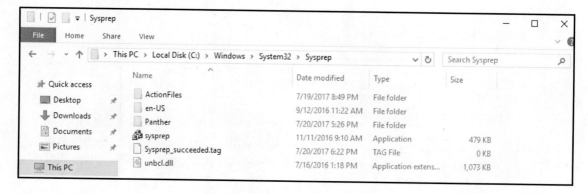

Figure 3.22: Sysprep path

2. Run `sysprep`, tick on the **Generalize** box, and select **Shutdown** in **Shutdown Options**, as shown in the following screenshot:

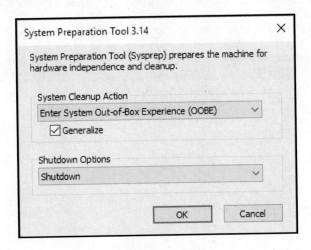

Figure 2.23: Running sysprep

3. Once you click on **OK**, sysprepping starts, as shown in the following screenshot:

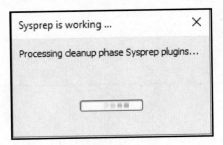

Figure 2.24: Syprepping

Now that you are done with sysprepping, the next step is to start capturing.

Capturing the VM with managed storage

This method is easier and very straightforward, as you will see in the following steps:

1. Navigate to the VM you want to capture, as shown in the following screenshot:

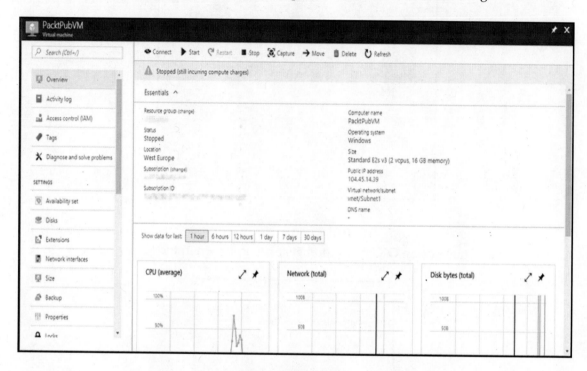

Figure 3.25: VM overview

2. Once you click on **Capture**, you will be navigated to another blade, asking you to specify the following parameters:
    *   **Name**: The image name
    *   **Resource group**: In which resource group put this image

- Whether you are willing to remove the VM after creating the image or not

Figure 2.26: Capturing a VM image

3. Once you click on **Create**, the process of capturing an image will start, and once this is done, you can find the image in **Images**, as shown in the following screenshot:

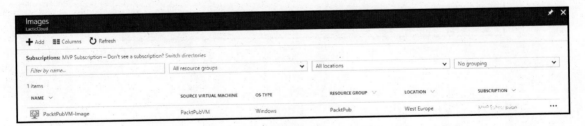

Figure 2.27: The captured image

Capturing the VM with unmanaged storage

This method is straightforward too, but you have to get the VM sysprepped first, and then follow these steps:

1. Navigate to **Images** and click on **Add**, and a new blade will open, as shown in the following screenshot:

Figure 2.28: Capturing a VM with unmanaged storage

2. All the fields to be filled in are pretty straightforward:
   - **Name**: The name of the image.
   - **Subscription**: The subscription that will be charged for storing the image.
   - **Resource group**: The resource group that the image will be assigned to.

- **Location**: Select the nearest location to you.
- **OS type**: Select the OS type of the VM, whether it is Windows or Linux.
- **Storage blob**: You will browse for the storage account in which the VM is stored, which will open a new blade for containers. Select the container in which the VM VHD is stored, then select the VM disk.
- **Account type**: Select the type of account, whether it is **Standard (HDD)** or **Premium**.
- **Host caching**: It is preferable to leave the host caching for the OS disk **Read/write**.
- **Data disks**: If you have any data disks that you want to attach to the VM image, you can click on **Add data disk** and add the disks you wish.

Figure 2.29: Capturing a VM image with unmanaged storage

For further information about managed and unmanaged disks, you can check the frequently asked questions posted by Microsoft via the following link: `https://docs.microsoft.com/en-us/azure/virtual-machines/windows/faq-for-disks`.

Automating the tasks

As usual at the end of each chapter, we get our hands dirty with automation.

Creating an Azure VM using PowerShell

Creating an Azure VM is one of the most common tasks on Azure, so let's get started.

First off, let's create the resources that make up the VM, and let's kick off with network resources.

Network resources

Every VM requires some network resources to be able to function properly, such as a subnet, virtual network, public IP address, and **network security group** (**NSG**), as shown in the following cmdlets:

```
$Subnet = New-AzureRmVirtualNetworkSubnetConfig -Name PacktPubSubnet -
AddressPrefix 10.0.0.0/24
$VirtualNetwork = New-AzureRmVirtualNetwork -ResourceGroupName PacktPub -
Location WestEurope -Name PacktPubvNet -AddressPrefix 10.0.0.0/8 -Subnet
$Subnet
$PIP = New-AzureRmPublicIpAddress -ResourceGroupName PacktPub -Location
WestEurope -AllocationMethod Dynamic -Name PacktPubVMPIP
```

Now we are done with the main network components, but the VM will require a firewall named **NSG** at Azure, so let's create an NSG with an inbound rule allowing us to RDP the VM, as shown in the following cmdlets:

```
$NSGRDPRule = New-AzureRmNetworkSecurityRuleConfig -Name PacktPubVMRDPRule
-Protocol TCP -Direction Inbound -Priority 1000 -SourceAddressPrefix * -
SourcePortRange * -DestinationAddressPrefix * -DestinationPortRange 3389 -
Access Allow
```

Where the priority number determines a higher priority for the rules and the lower the number the higher the priority, and `SourceAddressPrefix` is the range of IP address that would be able to connect to this VM. But, since we are connecting from on-premises, it could be any IP address, so in this case I selected *, which means any IP. However, you can determine a set of IP addresses that can access this VM. The same goes for `SourcePortRange`, but for ports, and the destination is completely the opposite for the source. Don't forget to determine whether this rule allows access or denies it:

```
$NSG = New-AzureRmNetworkSecurityGroup -Name "PacktPubNSG" -
ResourceGroupName PacktPub -Location WestEurope -SecurityRules $NSGRDPRule
```

Finally, let's create a `NIC` and assign it to all that we have created so far, as shown in the following cmdlets:

```
$NIC = New-AzureRmNetworkInterface -ResourceGroupName PacktPub -Location
WestEurope -Name PacktPubVMNIC -SubnetId $VirtualNetwork.Subnets[0].Id -
PublicIpAddressId $PIP.Id -NetworkSecurityGroupId $NSG.Id
```

VM configuration

Now, let's build up the main configuration for the VM, such as VM size, OS, computer name, the image, and so on, as shown in the following cmdlets:

```
$VMConfiguration = New-AzureRmVMConfig -VMName PacktPubVMPS -VMSize
Standard_D1_v2 | Set-AzureRmVMOperatingSystem -Windows -Credential (Get-
Credential) -ComputerName PackPubVMPS | Set-AzureRmVMSourceImage -
PublisherName MicrosoftWindowsServer -Offer WindowsServer -Skus 2016-
Datacenter -Version latest | Add-AzureRMVMNetworkInterface -Id $NIC.ID
```

- You can get all the sizes of the VM `Get-AzureRMVMSize -Location "specify the Location in which you are going to build your VM on"`
- You will be prompted to enter the VM credentials when you run the previous cmdlet

Creating the VM

Now, let's create the VM using the following cmdlet:

```
New-AzureRmVM -ResourceGroupName PacktPub -Location WestEurope -VM
$VMConfiguration
```

Creating an Azure VM using the Azure CLI 2.0

Creating an Azure VM using the Azure CLI 2.0 is pretty easy, and is only one command, shown as follows:

```
az vm create --resource-group PacktPub --name PacktPubVMCLI --location
westeurope --size Standard_DS2 --image win2016datacenter --storage-account
packtpubsacli --use-unmanaged-disk --vnet-name PacktPubvNet --vnet-address-
prefix 10.0.0.0/8 --subnet PacktPubSubnet --subnet-address-prefix
10.0.1.0/24 --admin-username pbuser --admin-password P@cktPub@2017
```

To get the available sizes of Azure VMs, run the following command:
`az vm list-sizes -l "the location in which you want to build your VM on"`.

Adding data disks to an Azure VM using PowerShell

Now, you have your VM up and running and want to add data disks to it using PowerShell, so you need to follow the following steps. The disk I am going to create is a managed disk:

1. First off, you have to specify the disk configuration, which will be used during the data disk creation, as shown in the following cmdlet:

```
$DiskConfiguration = New-AzureRmDiskConfig -Location
'West Europe' -DiskSizeGB 4095 -AccountType StandardLRS -OsType
Windows -CreateOption Empty
```

2. Once the configuration is created, you can start the creation of the data disk using the disk configuration variable for the disk parameter, as shown in the following cmdlet:

```
New-AzureRmDisk -ResourceGroupName PacktPub -DiskName
'PacktPub-DataDiskPS' -Disk $DiskConfiguration
```

3. Congratulations! You have a data disk, but it is useless, since it is not attached to any VMs, and that is what we are going to do in the following steps:

   1. Before attaching the disk to the VM, we have to create a PowerShell variable that retrieves Azure VM to which the data disks will be attached, as shown in the following cmdlet:

   ```
   $VM = Get-AzureRMVM -Name PacktPubVMPS -ResourceGroupName
   PacktPub
   ```

   2. Then, we can add the data disk to the VM, as shown in the following cmdlet:

   ```
   Add-AzureRmVMDataDisk -VM $VM -Name 'PacktPub-DataDiskPS'
   -Lun 0 -CreateOption Empty
   ```

You might wonder why I didn't put the VM name directly, instead of using a variable. Actually, this is because if you entered the VM name, it would be a `System.String` type and this cmdlet accepts the `Microsoft.Azure.Commands.Compute.Models.PSVirtualMachine` type, which has been accomplished by retrieving the VM name from a cmdlet of the same type.

   3. Finally, you have to save this configuration to the VM using the following cmdlet:

   ```
   Update-AzureRmVM -VM $VM -ResourceGroupName PacktPub
   ```

You cannot add a managed disk to a VM with blob-based disks, and vice versa.

Adding data disks to an Azure VM using the Azure CLI 2.0

The process of adding data disks using the Azure CLI 2.0 is pretty easy and can be done using only one command, shown as follows. The disk I am going to create is a managed disk:

```
az vm disk attach --vm-name PacktPubVMCLI --resource-group PacktPub --disk
PacktPub-DataDiskCLI --size-gb 4095 --new
```

Resizing Azure VM disks using PowerShell

Before starting the resizing process, you have to create a new disk and attach it to the VM we are working with. Then, using the same session, we will run the following cmdlets. The newly created disk name, in this case, is `PacktPub-DataDiskPS1` with a small size, so you can expand it:

```
$ResizeDisk = $VM.StorageProfile.DataDisks | Where {$_.Lun -eq 0 -and
$_.Name -eq "PacktPub-DataDiskPS1"}
$ResizeDisk.DiskSizeGB = 4095
Update-AzureRmVM -VM $VM -ResourceGroupName PacktPub
```

With the first variable, I specified which data disk I was going to resize and to which `Lun` it is assigned, then I resized it. Finally, I updated the VM to save the new configuration.

Resizing Azure VM disks using the Azure CLI 2.0

As we did when resizing using PowerShell, you have to first create a new disk with a small size, then run the following command:

```
az disk update --name PacktPub-DataDiskCLI1 --resource-group packtpub --
size-gb 4095
```

Changing the host caching using PowerShell

Changing the host caching is not a tough task. Using the same session, you can run the following cmdlet, which changes the caching mode of the disk from `None` to `ReadOnly`.

```
Set-AzureRmVMDataDisk -VM $VM -Name "PacktPub-DataDiskPS" -Caching ReadOnly
| Update-AzureRmVM
```

Changing the host caching using the Azure CLI 2.0

At the time of writing, you cannot change the host caching of a disk using the Azure CLI 2.0.

Capturing the VM using PowerShell

Before doing any PowerShell stuff, you have to sysprep the VM as we did earlier. Once it is sysprepped, run the following cmdlets:

```
Stop-AzureRmVM -ResourceGroupName PacktPub -Name PacktPubVMPS
Set-AzureRmVm -ResourceGroupName PacktPub -Name PacktPubVMPS -Generalized
Save-AzureRmVMImage -ResourceGroupName PacktPub -Name PacktPubVMPS -
DestinationContainerName vhds -VHDNamePrefix PacktPubImagePS
```

Capturing the VM using the Azure CLI 2.0

Again, you have to sysprep the VM by running the following commands:

```
az vm deallocate --resource-group PacktPub --name PacktPubVMCLI
az vm generalize --resource-group PacktPub --name PacktPubVMCLI
az image create --resource-group PacktPub --name PacktPubCLImage --source
PacktPubVMCLI
```

Further information

Azure VMs and Azure Storage could not be covered entirely in this chapter, however, it has covered most of the common topics you will deal with. For further information about Azure Storage for VMs, check out the following URLs:

- Migrating Azure VMs with unmanaged disks to managed disks: `https://docs.microsoft.com/en-us/azure/virtual-machines/windows/migrate-to-managed-disks`
- Disk snapshots: `https://docs.microsoft.com/en-us/azure/virtual-machines/windows/snapshot-copy-managed-disk`
- Backup Azure unmanaged VM disks with incremental snapshots: `https://docs.microsoft.com/en-us/azure/virtual-machines/windows/incremental-snapshots`
- Convert Azure managed disks storage from Standard to Premium and vice versa: `https://docs.microsoft.com/en-us/azure/virtual-machines/windows/convert-disk-storage`
- Migrate from **Amazon Web Services** (**AWS**) and other platforms to managed disks in Azure: `https://docs.microsoft.com/en-us/azure/virtual-machines/windows/on-prem-to-azure`

Summary

This has been a long and productive chapter, full of information and details. I've covered the most important topics about the relationship between Azure Storage and Azure VMs, which included what Azure VMs are, how to create them, and the key points to be considered about Azure Storage when creating VMs.

In the next chapter, we will cover a completely new topic--Azure SQL databases, how to work with them, and how to design a good solution in Azure.

4
Implementing Azure SQL Databases

In this chapter, we will go through one of the hottest topics, especially for **database administrators** (**DBAs**): Azure SQL Database. This chapter will be kicked off by an introduction to Azure SQL Database and why you should use this service, then the service tiers and performance level, which will be followed by some demonstrations of the Azure portal regarding how to create and restore Azure SQL Database. Finally, all the manual tasks we carry out in this chapter will be automated.

The following topics will be covered:

- An introduction to Azure SQL Database
- Why Azure SQL Database?
- Service tiers
- Creating an Azure SQL Database
- Connecting to Azure SQL Database
- Azure SQL Database business continuity
- Automating your common tasks with Azure SQL Database

An introduction to Azure SQL Database

A database is the most important component of most modern applications. Therefore, it is no surprise that we have two chapters of which I will cover most of the important key points and best practices for using Azure SQL Database.

Azure SQL Database is a relational database as a service, which means it follows the **Platform as a service (PaaS)** cloud service model, wherein you do not have to manage the underlying infrastructure, including networks, storage, servers, the virtualization layer, the operating system, middleware, or runtime. You only have to manage your databases and do not even have to think about patching and updating your servers.

Why Azure SQL Database?

Besides the reasons I've covered in the previous chapters as to why the cloud is always better than a traditional infrastructure, there are lots of other reasons for using Azure SQL Database, especially:

- **Scalability**: Azure SQL Database can be scaled according to your needs and usage, and more information about that topic will be covered later in the chapter.
- **Online scaling**: No downtime is needed to scale your database size. For example, you can start your application with a size that fits it in the beginning, and Azure SQL Database can respond to the database's requirements by scaling whenever necessary without causing any downtime.
- **Hardcore monitoring**: Azure SQL Database provides built-in monitoring and alerting tools that can be used to identify potential problems and even recommend actions to be taken in order to fix an issue. Alerts can also be generated based on the monitoring metrics, so you can receive an alert that something has gone wrong according to your baseline.
- **Built-in intelligence**: One of the coolest features of Azure SQL Database is built-in intelligence. It helps to reduce the costs involved in running databases and increases the performance of the application using Azure SQL Database as a backend.
- **Intelligent Threat Detection**: This feature utilizes SQL Database auditing in order to detect any harmful attempts to access data. It simply provides alerts for any abnormal behaviors.
- **High availability**: Microsoft provides many ways to ensure that Azure SQL Database is highly available:
    - **Automatic backup**: To avoid any issues that might cause data loss, automatic backups are performed on SQL Databases, (these include full, differential, and transaction log backups).
    - **Point-in-time restores**: Azure SQL Database can be recovered to any point-in-time within the automatic backup retention period.

- **Active geo-replication**: If you have an application that needs to be accessed from across the globe, you can use active geo-replication to avoid facing a high load on the original SQL Database. Azure geo-replication will create four secondary databases for the original database, with reading access.
- **Failover groups**: This feature is designed to help customers to recover from databases in secondary regions if a disaster occurs in the region that the original database is stored in.

This is a sneak peek of Azure SQL Database's most common features.

Service tiers

Azure SQL Database is available in two flavors:

- Elastic database pools
- Single databases

Elastic database pools

Elastic database pools are a great solution for managing multiple databases, scaling their performance according to the databases' needs, which means it is a good fit for databases with unpredictable usage demands, and that leads to a saving on credits. Elastic database pools share performance across many databases since all of these databases are built on a single Azure SQL Database server.

 At the time of writing, elastic database pools are generally available in all Azure regions, except in West India, as they are in the preview there. However, they will be generally available there too as soon as possible.

Single databases

Single databases are a good fit for a set of databases with predictable performance, where the required resources for the databases are predetermined.

Service tier types

At the time of writing, there are four service tiers for Azure SQL Database: Basic, Standard, Premium, and Premium RS (in preview). All of these offer support for elastic database pools and single databases. The performance of these tiers is expressed in **Database Transaction Units (DTUs)** for single databases, and **elastic Database Transaction Units (eDTUs)** for elastic database pools.

DTUs specify the performance for single databases, as they provide a specific amount of resources to that database.

On the other hand, eDTUs do not provide a dedicated set of resources for a database, as they share resources within a specific Azure SQL Server to all the databases which run that server.

For more information about DTUs and eDTUs, you can check out the following article:
`https://docs.microsoft.com/en-us/azure/sql-database/sql-database-what-is-a-dtu`
. To calculate your required DTUs, especially when you are migrating an on-premises SQL Server database, you can use the Azure SQL DTU calculator, which can be accessed from the following link: `http://dtucalculator.azurewebsites.net/`.

The following is a table from Microsoft which illustrates the different tiers' performance levels for elastic databases pools:

	Basic	Standard	Premium	Premium RS
Maximum storage size per database	2 GB	1 TB	1 TB	1 TB
Maximum storage size per pool	156 GB	4 TB	4 TB	1 TB
Maximum eDTUs per database	5	3,000	4,000	1,000
Maximum eDTUs per pool	1,600	3,000	4,000	1,000
Maximum number of databases per pool	500	500	100	100

The following is a table that illustrates the different tiers' performance levels for single databases:

	Basic	Standard	Premium	Premium RS
Maximum storage size	2 GB	1 TB	4 TB	1 TB
Maximum DTUs	5	3,000	4,000	1,000

Reference: `https://docs.microsoft.com/en-us/azure/sql-database-service-tiers#choosing-a-service-tier`.

- For a detailed comparison of performance levels for single databases, you can check out the following link: `https://docs.microsoft.com/en-us/azure/sql-database/sql-database-resource-limits#single-database-storage-sizes-and-performance-levels`
- For a detailed comparison of performance levels of elastic database pools, you can check out the following link: `https://docs.microsoft.com/en-us/azure/sql-database/sql-database-resource-limits#elastic-pool-storage-sizes-and-performance-levels`

Creating an Azure SQL Database

To create an Azure SQL Database via the Azure portal, perform the following steps:

1. Navigate to the Azure portal, then to **More services**, and search for SQL Databases, as shown in the following screenshot:

Figure 4.1: Searching for Azure SQL Database

2. When you open **SQL databases**, a new blade pops up, and if there're any SQL Databases that you created earlier, they will be displayed here. But since no SQL Databases have been created so far, it will be blank, as shown in the following screenshot:

Figure 4.2: Azure SQL Database blade

3. To create a new Azure SQL Database, click on **Add**, or **Create SQL databases**.

4. Once you have done so, a new blade will pop up, as shown in the following
   screenshot:

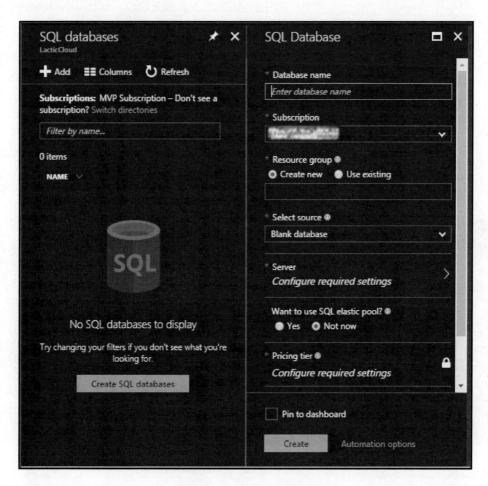

Figure 4.3: Creating a new SQL Database

The fields in this demonstration will be filled in as follows:

- **Database name**: PacktPubDB.
- **Subscription**: Select the subscription you are planning to assign
  this resource to.
- **Resource group**: **PacktPub** resource group will be used to store
  this resource.

- **Select source**: There are three options for selecting the source:
  - **Blank database**: This will create a new database, which will be built from scratch by you (this is the selected option for this demonstration)
  - **Sample (AdventureWorksLT)**: This is a sample database, and if chosen, it loads the AdventureWorks schema and data into your new database
  - **Backup**: If you want to restore any backed up database on Azure, this option fits that situation
- **Server**: Specify the SQL Server on which you are going to build this SQL Database. If you have no SQL Servers already built, you will have to build a new one, as shown in the following screenshot:

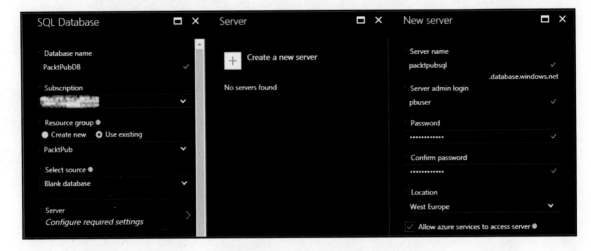

Figure 4.4: Creating an SQL Server to host SQL Databases

 By default, all Azure services have access to this SQL Server, which means there will be no need to open ports for communication with other Azure services.

- **Want to use an SQL elastic pool?** For now, I'll select **Not now**, which means you will be using a single database type.
- **Pricing tier**: You can choose the pricing tier that suits you from the varying set of tiers that were covered earlier. Remember that you can change the DTUs and storage allocated to the database to the limits of every tier. Also, the costs of the DTUs and storage will be displayed next to it, as shown in the following screenshot:

Figure 4.5: Selecting the desired service tier and the desired performance configuration

- **Collation**: Finally, you can specify the collation that suits you. Remember that you have to first check whether the application that will used will support this collation for the SQL or not.

5. Once you are done, you can click on **Create**, as shown in the following screenshot:

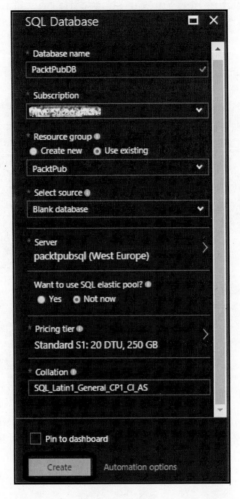

Figure 4.6: Creating an SQL Server Database

6. Since this database will be built upon a new SQL Server, it will take a little while to be created, but if it is built upon a pre-created SQL Server, it will take almost no time at all. Once the database is created, you can navigate to the **SQL database** blade to check it, as shown in the following screenshot:

Figure 4.7: Overview of the created SQL Database

7. You can also check that the SQL Server that hosts this database has been created by navigating to the **SQL servers** blade, as shown in the following screenshot:

Figure 4.8: Overview of the created SQL Server

Connecting to Azure SQL Database

As mentioned earlier, when you create an Azure Database via the Azure portal, all Azure services will be allowed to access this database with no further configuration.

However, when you want to connect to the database from anywhere else, there is some configuration that needs to be done.

Server-level firewall rule

To allow access to an Azure SQL Database from somewhere else, you will have to set a server-level firewall rule, as described in the following steps:

1. Navigate to the database blade, and click on **Set server firewall**, as shown in the following figure:

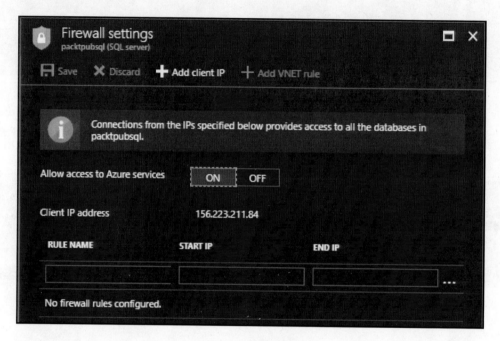

Figure 4.9: PacktPubDB settings

2. Once you have clicked on it, you will be navigated to a new blade, where you can create firewall rules for the Azure SQL Server, as shown in the following screenshot:

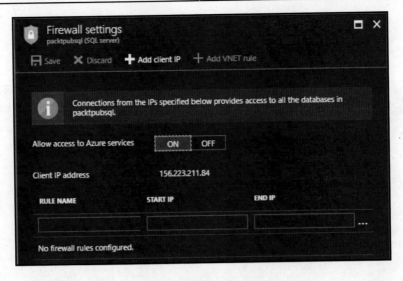

Figure 4.10: Azure SQL Server firewall settings

3. Within this blade, you can add IP addresses that have access to the database we created earlier. This can be done either as an IP address range, where you can specify **START IP** and **END IP**, or as a single IP address, written the same as in **START IP** and **END IP**. But, since I need to connect to this database via my client (laptop), I'll directly click on **Add client IP**, which will be automatically loaded, and as a rule with a default name, as shown in the following screenshot:

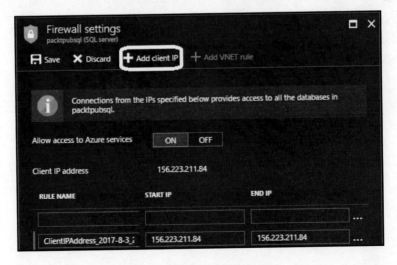

Figure 4.11: Creating a server firewall rule

4. Once you are done with the IP address that will be allowed to access the database, click on **Save**, and it should take no longer than two seconds for a success message to be displayed, as shown in the following screenshot:

Figure 4.12: Updating the firewall settings

Now, you are good to go. You can connect to the database via your client.

Make sure that port 1433 is open in your environment, which is used for communication between the SQL Server and the client (**Server Management Studio (SSMS)**).

Connecting to Azure SQL Database using SQL SSMS

To connect to the created database via SQL Server Management Studio, you can follow these steps:

1. Navigate to the database blade and copy **Server name**, as shown in the following screenshot:

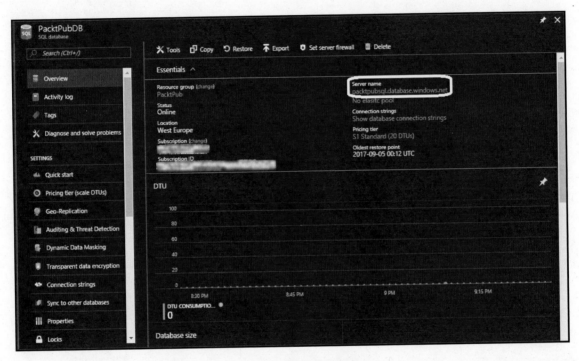

Figure 4.13: Overview of the PacktPubDB

2. Open SSMS, paste the name of the server, change the **Authentication** to **SQL Server Authentication**, and enter the SQL Server credentials that you entered during the SQL Server creation, as shown in the following screenshot:

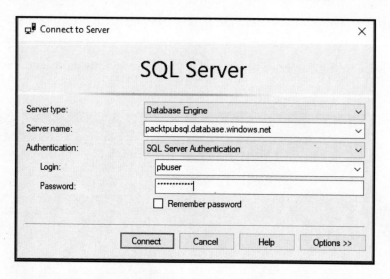

Figure 4.14: Connecting to an Azure SQL Database via SSMS

3. Once you click on **Connect**, you will be connected to your database on Azure, as shown in the following screenshot:

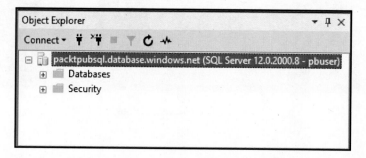

Figure 4.15: The database created on Azure displayed via SSMS

 You can create firewall rules at the database level as we have done at the server level. However, these rules can only be created using Transact-SQL. For further information about how to do so, you can check the following link: https://docs.microsoft.com/en-us/azure/sql-database/sql-database-firewall-configure.

Azure SQL Database business continuity

So far, you have your database up and running on the cloud, and you can even connect to it, create, delete, and update the tables as you wish.

I think that should satisfy most of your needs, but since a database is something critical and you need to make sure that it will not be lost if corruption occurs, you will need to take some backups.

Unfortunately, when you check the database blade, you will notice that backup is not mentioned in the blade, as shown in the following screenshot:

Figure 4.16: Azure SQL Database blade settings

How business continuity works for Azure SQL Database

Microsoft does its best to address any issues that might occur with Azure SQL Database, and it provides the following solutions for this purpose.

Hardware failure

Hardware failure is something that is expected to happen, but it will not be the reason you lose your databases.

Just as there is replication provided for storage, as mentioned in `Chapter 1`, *Understanding Azure Storage 101*, there is something similar to it for Azure databases.

If the hardware failure occurs, there are three copies of your database separated across three physical nodes. The three copies consist of one primary replica and two secondary replicas, and in order to avoid any data loss, write operations are not committed in the primary replica until they have been committed in one of the secondary replicas. Therefore, whenever a hardware failure occurs, it will failover to the secondary replica.

Point-in-time restore

As mentioned earlier, point-in-time restores can recover Azure SQL Database at any point in time within the automatic backup retention period. The retention period varies from one tier to another: 7 days for the Basic tier, 35 days for the Standard tier, 35 days for the Premium tier, and 35 days for the Premium RS tier. This solution would suit a scenario where your database has been corrupted and you want to restore it to the last healthy point.

To restore your database to the last healthy point, you have to follow these steps:

1. Navigate to the database you want to restore to the last point, as shown in the following screenshot:

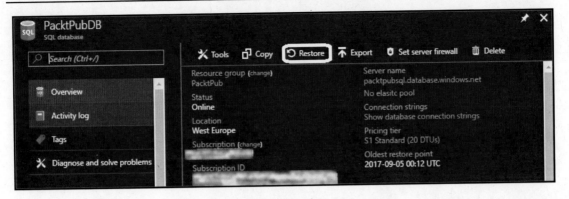

Figure 4.17: Restoring Azure SQL Database

2. Once you have clicked on **Restore**, a new blade will pop up, where you can give the restored database a new database name, determine the time that you want to restore to, and change the pricing tier for the restored database, as shown in the following screenshot:

Figure 4.18: Azure SQL Database restore settings

3. Once you click on **OK**, it starts restoring the database, as shown in the following screenshot:

Figure 4.19: The database is being restored

Restoring Azure SQL Database key points

For a better understanding of the process, you should consider the following key points during implementation:

- When you restore a database, a new database will be created, which means you will have to pay for the new database too
- You cannot name the new database with the same name as the original database because the original still exists; to do so you would have to remove the original one
- You can choose a restore point between the earliest point and the latest backup time, which is six minutes before the current time
- Database recovery time varies from one database to another according to many factors; here are some of them:
  - The database size
  - The number of transaction logs involved in the operations
  - The database performance level
  - If you are restoring the database from a different region, the network bandwidth might cause a delay

Restoring a deleted database

You can accidentally remove a database, or you might have removed a database and figured out later that you need it. This can be a tough situation. However, Microsoft Azure supports database recovery even in the case of deletion, but the SQL Server on which the database was built cannot have been deleted because, at the time of writing, there is no support for the recovery of deleted SQL Servers.

To restore a deleted database, follow these steps:

1. Navigate to SQL Servers and select the server on which the deleted database was built.
2. Scroll down to **Deleted databases** in the SQL Server blade, as shown in the following screenshot:

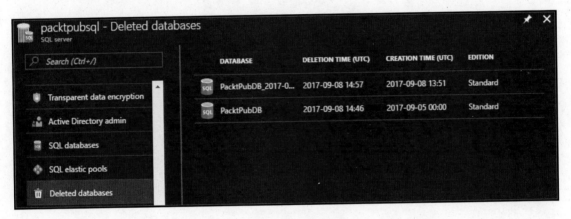

Figure 4.20: The deleted databases

3. Select the database you want to restore and name it as you wish, considering that you cannot give the name of an existing database that is already running on the same SQL Server, but you can give it its old name, as shown in the following screenshot:

Figure 4.21: Restore the deleted database

4. Once you are done, you can click on **OK**, and it will start the restoration process.

Geo-restore

Geo-restore provides a backup restore for the SQL Server in a new region and will be covered in detail in the coming chapter.

Automating the tasks

As usual, at the end of each chapter, we get our hands dirty with automation.

Creating an Azure SQL Database using PowerShell

First off, you will have to create the SQL Server on which the database will be built, and since the SQL Server needs an admin name and a password, they will be created and stored in variables:

```
$SQLAdmin = "SQL Admin User Name"
$Password = "SQL Admin Password"
```

Then, you can work on creating the SQL Server with the following cmdlets:

```
New-AzureRmSqlServer -ResourceGroupName PacktPub -ServerName packtpubsqlps
-Location WestEurope -SqlAdministratorCredentials $(New-Object -TypeName
System.Management.Automation.PSCredential -ArgumentList
$SQLAdmin,$(ConvertTo-SecureString -String $Password -AsPlainText -Force))
```

Once you are done with the SQL Server, you can create the database on it:

```
New-AzureRmSqlDatabase -ResourceGroupName PacktPub -ServerName
packtpubsqlps -DatabaseName PackPubDBPS -RequestedServiceObjectiveName "S3"
-CollationName "SQL_Latin1_General_CP1_CI_AS"
```

Where `RequestedServiceObjectiveName` is the performance level.

When you create an Azure SQL Server via PowerShell, access from other Azure services to that SQL Server is not allowed by default.

Creating an Azure SQL Database using the Azure CLI 2.0

To create an Azure SQL Database using the Azure CLI 2.0, we have to create an Azure SQL Server first, which can be done by running the following command:

```
az sql server create --name packtpubsqlcli --resource-group PacktPub --
location westeurope --admin-user "SQL Admin User" --admin-password "SQL
Admin Password"
```

Then, the following command will be run to create the database:

```
az sql db create --resource-group PacktPub --server packtpubsqlcli --name
PacktPubDBCLI --service-objective S3 --collation
SQL_Latin1_General_CP1_CI_AS
```

When you create an Azure SQL Server via the Azure CLI 2.0, access from other Azure services to that SQL Server is not allowed by default.

Creating an SQL Server-level firewall rule using PowerShell

To allow access to databases built on the SQL Server, some firewall rules need to be made, and to do so, you have to run the following cmdlet:

```
New-AzureRmSqlServerFirewallRule -ResourceGroupName PacktPub -ServerName
packtpubsqlps -FirewallRuleName "Name the Rule" -StartIpAddress
XXX.XXX.XXX.XXX -EndIpAddress XXX.XXX.XXX.XXX
```

Creating an SQL Server-level firewall rule using Azure CLI 2.0

Creating an SQL Server-level firewall rule using the Azure CLI 2.0 is pretty straightforward, as we did in PowerShell. To do so, you have to run the following command:

```
az sql server firewall-rule create --resource-group PacktPub --server
packtpubsqlcli --name PPRule --start-ip-address XXX.XXX.XXX.XXX --end-ip-
address XXX.XXX.XXX.XXX
```

Point-in-time restore using PowerShell

First off, we have to create two variables, one for the database properties, and the other for the date to which we want to restore the database to:

```
$Database = Get-AzureRmSqlDatabase -ResourceGroupName PacktPub -ServerName
packtpubsqlps -DatabaseName PacktPubDBPS
$ Date = Get-Date - Date "The date you want to restore to"
$Date = $Date.ToUniversalTime()
```

Then, you can start the restoration process by triggering the following cmdlet:

```
Restore-AzureRmSqlDatabase -FromPointInTimeBackup -PointInTime $Date -
ResourceGroupName PacktPub -ServerName packtpubsqlps -TargetDatabaseName
"PacktPubRestoredDB" -ServiceObjectiveName "S3" -ResourceId
$Database.ResourceId
```

Point-in-time restore using the Azure CLI 2.0

At the time of writing, you cannot do this using the Azure CLI 2.0.

Restoring a deleted database using PowerShell

Using the same method that we used to restore a point-in-time database, a deleted database is restored with only a few minor changes, as shown in the following cmdlets:

```
$DeletedDatabase = Get-AzureRmSqlDeletedDatabaseBackup -ResourceGroupName
PacktPub -ServerName packtpubsqlps -DatabaseName PacktPubDBPS
$Date = Get-Date - Date "The date you want to restore to"
$Date = $Date.ToUniversalTime()
Restore-AzureRmSqlDatabase -FromDeletedDatabaseBackup -DeletionDate
$DeletedDatabase.DeletionDate -ResourceGroupName
$DeletedDatabase.ResourceGroupName -ServerName packtpubsqlps -
TargetDatabaseName "RestoredDatabase-Deleted" -ResourceId
$DeletedDatabase.ResourceID -ServiceObjectiveName "S3" -PointInTime $Date
```

Where the point-in-time parameter is the time you want to restore your database to.

Restoring a deleted database using PowerShell

At the time of writing, you cannot do this task using the Azure CLI 2.0.

Summary

So far, we have covered basic concepts about Azure SQL Database and the reasons to use them. In addition, we looked at an overview of service tiers and performance levels, which will help with designing your database solution. Also, some demonstrations were implemented in order to have a better understanding of what is going on when you deal with things in Azure.

Next, some topics that have been mentioned in this chapter and some of the main concerns, such as security, will be covered in more detail in the coming chapter.

5
Beyond Azure SQL Database Management

In this chapter, we are continuing the journey of working with Azure SQL Databases, and since SQL Servers can be implemented using two service models (**Infrastructure as a Service (IaaS)** and **Platform as a Service (PaaS)**), we'll kick off the chapter by illustrating the difference between them, followed by covering elastic database pools, then demonstrating how to set Azure **Active Directory (AD)** authentication on Azure SQL Databases.

Since the availability of your databases is very important, and you want to avoid losing them even in the event of a disaster, you have to embrace active geo-replication, which will not only play a role in ensuring that doesn't happen but will also help you to build a globally distributed application. The concept of doing so and how to do so is covered in detail later in the chapter. Finally, you will learn how to automate all of the manual tasks that are done throughout the chapter.

The following topics will be covered:

- SQL Databases (IaaS/PaaS)
- Azure SQL elastic database pools
- Setting Azure AD authentication to Azure SQL Database
- Active geo-replication
- Automating manual tasks

SQL Database (IaaS/PaaS)

An SQL Database can be implemented in Azure in two ways:

- **Using Azure SQL Database**: It follows the PaaS model, and we have been using it so far
- **Using Azure VMs and building SQL on them**: This follows an IaaS model, and will be covered in more detail shortly

Azure SQL Database (PaaS)

As mentioned earlier, Azure SQL Database is a relational database as a service, built and hosted on Azure.

Azure SQL Database minimizes the costs of managing and provisioning databases. Using this model will reduce the responsibility of managing the virtual machines that host the SQL server, the operating system, and even the SQL Server software.

This model eliminates concerns regarding upgrades, backups, and even the high availability of databases, because they are not your responsibility anymore, in addition to being able to add databases as you wish, whenever you want. Taking this into account, you will pay less credits because, in this scenario, you will not pay for a VM with SQL installed on it, plus the license credits; you will only pay for the database you are using.

Scenarios that would fit in Azure SQL Database

Azure SQL Database would be a best fit for the following scenarios:

- Cloud applications that need to be developed quickly
- Building a highly-available and auto-upgradable database that is recoverable in the event of disasters
- A database with less management needed for its OS and configuration
- Building a **Software as a service (SaaS)** application
- If you want complete management of your SQL installation, but no worries about hardware

SQL on Azure VMs (IaaS)

This type of deployment of an SQL Server is much more complicated than using Azure SQL Database, as a VM built on Azure and an SQL Server built upon it requires more administration. Also, you can use whichever versions you want to use (2008R2, 2012, 2014, 2016, 2017), and whichever edition you need (Developer, Express, Web, Standard, or Enterprise).

Scenarios that would suit SQL on Azure VMs

The following scenarios would be the best fit for building SQL on Azure VMs:

- Migrating existing apps on-premises to Azure with minimal changes
- Having a SQL environment wherein you have full access to it
- Needing databases of up to 64 TB storage, since Azure SQL Database can support only up to 4 TB
- Building hybrid applications with SQL Database as a backend

Azure SQL elastic database pools

In the previous chapter, some interesting and important topics were covered regarding elastic database pools. In this section, we will be working on creating and managing elastic database pools.

Creating an elastic database pool

To get your elastic database pool up and running, you have to follow these steps:

1. Navigate to the **SQL databases** blade, and click on **Add** or **Create SQL databases**, as shown in the following screenshot:

Figure 5.1: SQL Databases blade

2. Once you have clicked on **Add** or **Create SQL databases**, a new blade will pop up, as shown in the following screenshot:

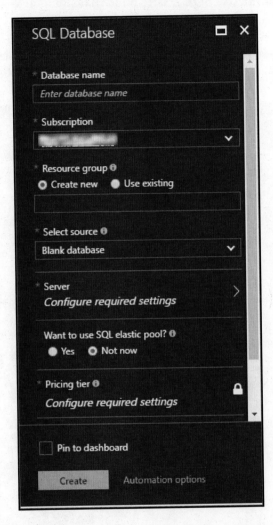

Figure 5.2: Create a new SQL Database blade

3. Since most of the required fields were covered in the previous chapter, only changed options will be covered:

    1. **Want to use SQL elastic pool?**: This will be **Yes** this time.

    2. Once **Yes** is selected, **Pricing tier** option, which is shown in the preceding screenshot, will be changed to **Elastic database pool**, where it will ask you to configure the pool setting. Once you have clicked on it, a new blade will pop up, as shown in the following screenshot:

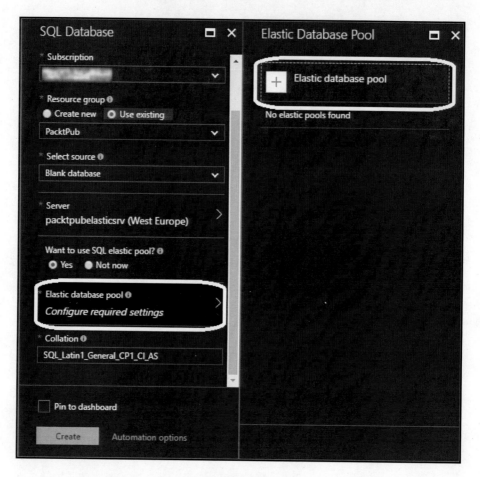

Figure 5.3: Configuring elastic database pool settings

3. Once you have clicked on **Elastic database pool**, a new blade will pop up, as shown in the following screenshot:

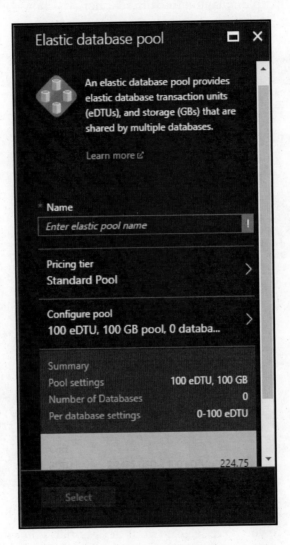

Figure 5.4: Creating an elastic database pool

4. You can name the elastic pool as you wish. To determine the pricing tier you are going to select, click on **Pricing tier** and a new blade will pop up displaying the different tiers, as shown in the following screenshot:

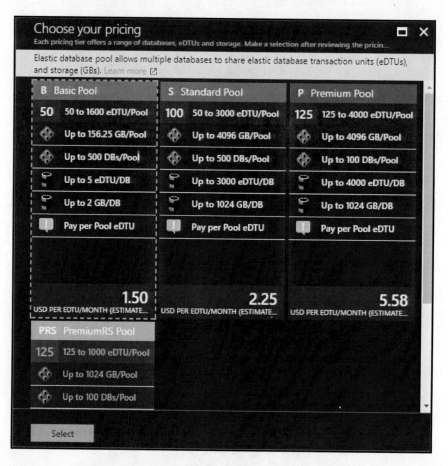

Figure 5.5: Selecting the pricing tier for an elastic database pool

5. Once you have selected your desired tier, you can open the **Configure pool** blade, where you can specify **Pool eDTU**, **Pool GB** (which are the reserved **elastic Database Transaction Units (eDTUs)**), and the maximum storage capacity of GB for the pool. Take into consideration that the ratio of eDTU to GB is determined by the pricing tier, as shown in the following screenshot:

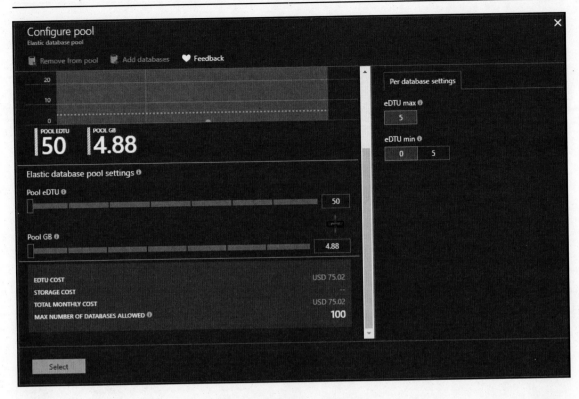

Figure 5.6: Configuring an elastic database pool

6. Once you are done, click on **Select** for the pool, and in the **Elastic database pool** blade too.

4. Finally, click on **Create**.

5. Once it is done with deployment, you will find the newly created database in the **SQL databases** blade, as shown in the following screenshot:

Figure 5.7: The created SQL Database

Adding a database to the elastic database pool

Once you get your elastic database pool up and running, you can add databases to it, and to do so, you need to follow these steps:

1. Navigate to the **SQL servers** blade and click on the SQL Server created earlier to be able to add new databases to it, as shown in the following screenshot:

Figure 5.8: The Azure SQL Server that hosts the elastic databases pool

2. There are two ways to add databases to the pool according to the preceding screenshot:
    - **New database**: In this case, you will go through the same steps we did earlier
    - **Import database**: In this case, you will import an existing database to be added to the pool

3. In this demonstration, adding a new database will be covered. Therefore, we will click on **New database.**

4. Once you have clicked on it, a new blade will pop up and you will have to determine whether you want to use an elastic database pool or not. If you do, you will have to specify which pool it should be added to until you have filled in all the fields, as shown in the following screenshot:

Figure 5.9: Adding an additional database to the pool

5. Once you are done, click **OK**, and the database will be created in seconds.

Setting Azure AD authentication to Azure SQL Database

So far, we have been using SQL authentication to connect to Azure SQL Database, as we did in the previous chapter via SQL Server Management Studio.

Using Azure AD will provide centralized administration for database users' identities.

Doing so is very straightforward; you can follow the following steps to do so:

1. Navigate to the Azure SQL Server and scroll down to **Active Directory admin**, as shown in the following screenshot:

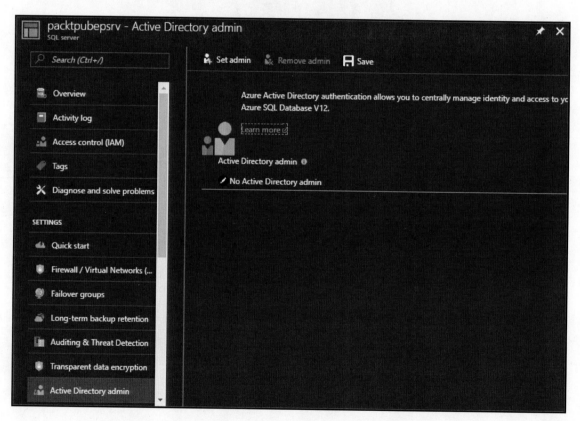

Figure 5.10: Azure AD admins for the Azure SQL Server

2. Click on **Set admin** and a new blade will pop up, as shown in the following screenshot:

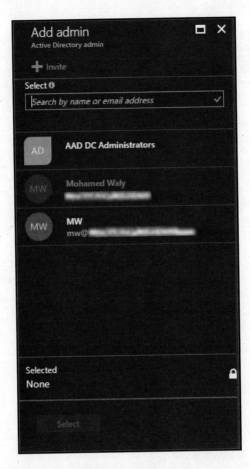

Figure 5.11: Azure AD users and groups

3. Select the desired user or group to be added as an AD admin on the SQL Server, then save your changes to be applied to the SQL Server, as shown in the following screenshot:

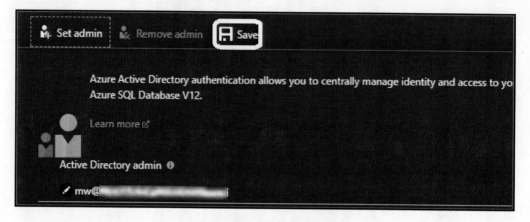

Figure 5.12: Saving changes to the SQL Server

4. After saving the changes, open SSMS and change **Authentication** from **SQL Server Authentication** to **Active Directory – Universal with MFA support**, as shown in the following screenshot:

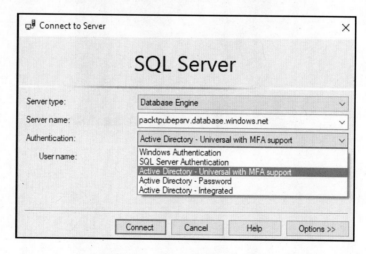

Figure 5.13: Changing the authentication method to Azure SQL Database via SSMS

5. Then, provide the username of the Azure AD you have set as admin and click on **Connect**. A new wizard will pop up asking for the user's password, as shown in the following screenshot:

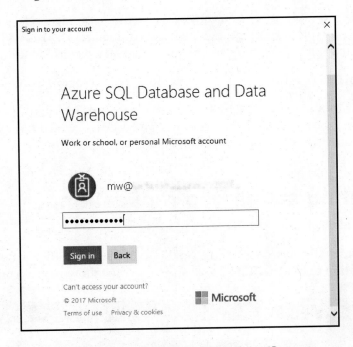

Figure 5.14: Signing in to Azure SQL Database using an Azure AD user

6. Once you are signed in, you can start getting your hands dirty with your databases, as shown in the following screenshot:

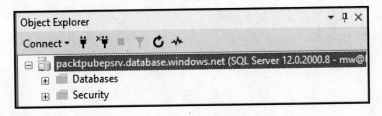

Figure 5.15: Managing Azure SQL Database via SSMS

At the time of writing, you cannot connect to SQL Database hosted on Azure VMs using Azure AD. It is only supported for Azure SQL Database. For more information about Azure AD, you can check out the following link: `https://docs.microsoft.com/en-us/azure/active-directory/`.

Active geo-replication

Active geo-replication is one of the most important business continuity methodologies.

When using active geo-replication, you can configure up to four secondary databases within the same region or in different regions with reading access. This will help to reduce latency for users or applications that need to query the database from a different region.

If a catastrophic disaster occurs, you can failover to the other region using a failover group.

Failover groups are mainly designed to manage every aspect of geo-replication automatically, such as connectivity, relationships, and failover. Considering that it is enabled across Azure SQL Database Basic and Standard service tiers.

Implementing active geo-replication

To get active geo-replication implemented, follow these steps:

1. Navigate to the desired database on the Azure portal and click on **Geo-Replication** under **SETTINGS**, as shown in the following screenshot:

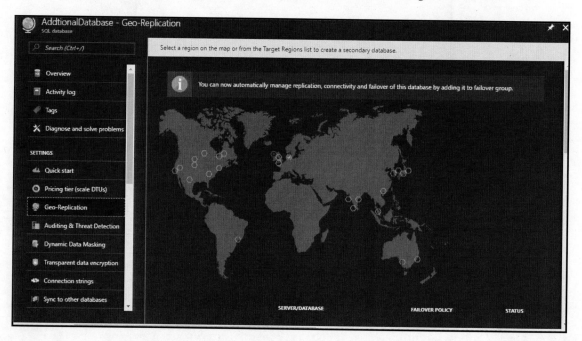

Figure 5.16: Active geo-replication

2. Click on the region you want to replicate to.

3. Once the region is selected, a new blade will pop up asking you to configure the secondary server for which the database will be replicated to, as shown in the following screenshot:

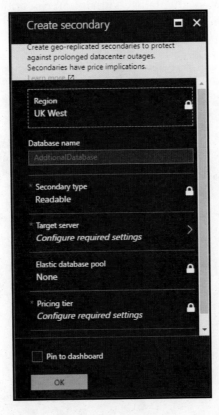

Figure 5.17: Configuring the secondary server

4. When it comes to specifying the **Target server**, you can either create a new Azure SQL Server in the new region or select one that already exists there.

5. Once you are done, it starts deploying the new Azure SQL Server and migrates the database to it.

Adding the databases to a failover group

Once the deployment of active geo-replication is done, you can start adding databases to a failover group by following these steps:

1. Click on the statement that tells you that you can add the database to a failover group, as shown in the following screenshot:

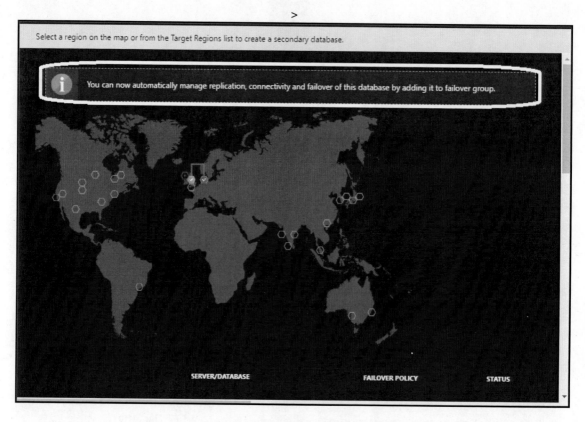

Figure 5.18: Adding databases to a failover group

2. Once you have clicked on it, you will be navigated to another blade asking you to specify the following configurations:
   - **Secondary server**: Specify the secondary server that hosts the replicated database
   - **Failover group name**: Specify a descriptive name for the failover group

- **Read/Write failover policy**: You can let that process be done automatically, which is the default and is recommended, or manually do it yourself
- **Read/Write grace period (hours)**: Specify the time between every automatic failover

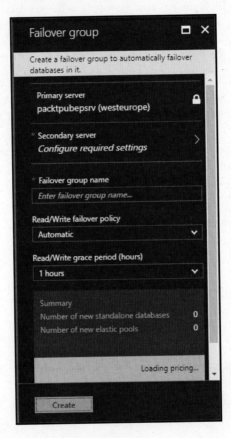

Figure 5.19: Configuring failover group

3. Once you are done, click on **Create** and the failover group should be deployed

Active geo-replication key points

For a better design for your solution when using active geo-replication, you have to consider the following key points:

- Replication between a primary database and a secondary database is asynchronous, which means that the data will be committed to the primary database before being replicated to the secondary database.
- Primary and secondary databases must have the same service tier (Basic, Standard, Premium, or Premium RS).
- Although it is technically valid to have lower **Database Transaction Units** (**DTUs**) in the secondary database than the primary, it is not recommended to do so, because that would increase the replication lag for apps with intensive write operations.
- When replicating databases from within an elastic databases pool to another region, they can be replicated to another elastic databases pool.
- Single databases can be replicated to an elastic databases pool if the service tiers are the same.
- You are only allowed to have four readable secondary databases. However, you can get more than that, especially if you have a globally distributed application, by creating a secondary database from the secondary database, which is known as chaining.
- When you add a database to a failover group, it automatically creates a secondary database with the same specifications.

Automating the tasks

As usual, at the end of each chapter, we get our hands dirty with automation.

Creating an elastic database pool using PowerShell

To create an elastic database pool, you must have an Azure SQL Server. You can use the one created in the previous chapter using PowerShell or create a new one yourself.

Then, you can run the following cmdlet to build an elastic database pool:

```
New-AzureRmSqlElasticPool -ResourceGroupName PacktPub -ServerName
"packtpubsqlps" -ElasticPoolName "EDPPS" -Dtu 400 -DatabaseDtuMin 10 -
DatabaseDtuMax 100
```

Where:

- `-Dtu` is the maximum number of eDTUs in the pool
- `-DatabaseDtuMin` is the minimum number of eDTUs assigned to a database
- `-DatabaseDtuMax` is the maximum number of eDTUs assigned to a database

Creating an elastic database pool using Azure CLI 2.0

To create an elastic database pool, you must have an Azure SQL Server. You can use the one created in the previous chapter using the Azure CLI 2.0 or create a new one yourself:

```
az sql elastic-pool create --resource-group PacktPub --server
packtpubsqlcli --name EDPCLI --dtu 400 --db-dtu-min 10 --db-dtu-max 100
```

Adding database to the elastic database pool using PowerShell

To add a database to the created elastic pool, run the following cmdlet:

```
New-AzureRmSqlDatabase -ResourceGroupName PacktPub -ServerName
"packtpubsqlps" -DatabaseName "additionaldbps" -ElasticPoolName "EDPPS"
```

Adding an additional database to the elastic database pool using Azure CLI 2.0

To add a database to the created elastic pool, run the following command:

```
az sql db create --resource-group PacktPub --server packtpubsqlcli --name
additionaldbcli --elastic-pool edpcli
```

Setting Azure AD authentication to Azure SQL Database using PowerShell

To set authentication to Azure SQL Database using Azure AD users, you have to run the following cmdlet:

```
Set-AzureRmSqlServerActiveDirectoryAdministrator -ResourceGroupName PacktPub
-ServerName packtpubsqlps -DisplayName "x@x.com"
```

Setting Azure AD authentication to Azure SQL Database using the Azure CLI 2.0

To set authentication to Azure SQL Database using Azure AD users, you have to run the following command:

```
az sql server ad-admin create --resource-group PacktPub --server-name
packtpubsqlcli --display-name x@x.com --object-id "Enter the object id of
Azure AD Admin"
```

To get the object ID of a specific user, run the following command:

```
az ad user show --upn x@x.com
```

Implementing active geo-replication using PowerShell

First off, you have to create a secondary server in another region, and if the database is built on an elastic database pool, you have to create the elastic database pool on the other server, then run the following command to establish active geo-replication:

```
Get-AzureRmSqlDatabase -DatabaseName additionaldbps -ResourceGroupName
PacktPub -ServerName packtpubsqlpssec | New-AzureRmSqlDatabaseSecondary -
PartnerResourceGroupName PacktPub -PartnerServerName packtpubsqlpssec -
AllowConnections "All"
```

Implementing active geo-replication using Azure CLI 2.0

At the time of writing, implementing active geo-replication is not available via the Azure CLI 2.0.

Adding databases to a failover group using PowerShell

First off, you will have to create a failover group by running the following cmdlet:

```
New-AzureRMSqlDatabaseFailoverGroup -ResourceGroupName PacktPub -ServerName
packtpubsqlps -PartnerServerName packtpubsqlpssec -FailoverGroupName psfg
-FailoverPolicy Automatic -GracePeriodWithDataLossHours 1 | Add-
AzureRmSqlDatabaseToFailoverGroup -ResourceGroupName PacktPub -ServerName
packtpubsqlps -FailoverGroupName psfg
```

Then, you can add the database to the failover group by running the following cmdlet:

```
Get-AzureRmSqlDatabase -ResourceGroupName PacktPub -ServerName
packtpubsqlps -DatabaseName additionaldbps | Add-
AzureRmSqlDatabaseToFailoverGroup -ResourceGroupName PacktPub -ServerName
packtpubsqlps -FailoverGroupName psfg
```

Adding databases to a failover group using the Azure CLI 2.0

At the time of writing, adding databases to a failover group is not available via the Azure CLI 2.0.

Further information

Most of the important and commonly used features of Azure SQL Database have been covered in the last two chapters. However, for further information about other topics related to Azure SQL Database that has not been covered, you can check out the following links:

- **Monitoring and tuning performance**: https://docs.microsoft.com/en-us/azure/sql-database/sql-database-troubleshoot-performance
- **Scaling out with Azure SQL Database**: https://docs.microsoft.com/en-us/azure/sql-database/sql-database-elastic-scale-introduction
- **SQL Server Database migration to SQL Database in the cloud**: https://docs.microsoft.com/en-us/azure/sql-database/sql-database-cloud-migrate
- **Securing Azure SQL Database**: https://docs.microsoft.com/en-us/azure/sql-database/sql-database-security-overview

Summary

This chapter has been an extension of the previous one, and throughout the chapter, very important things have been brought to the table to illustrate the use of Azure SQL Database also fulfilling the need to design globally distributed applications.

In the next chapter, we will work on one of the most important features of Azure, which is Azure Backup. This feature has become much more important recently, especially since the recent ransomware attacks.

6
Azure Backup

In this chapter, you will learn about Azure Backup and why it is so important. Then, we will move forward to cover the pre-configurations for the backup process and how to do a backup on Azure. After that, you will learn how to store files on Azure Virtual Machines. Finally, you will learn how to automate the manual tasks that are implemented throughout the chapter.

The following topics will be covered:

- An introduction to Azure Backup
- Why Azure Backup?
- The process of backing up data
- Further information
- Automating tasks

An introduction to Azure Backup

Backup has always been the X factor that saves an environment from being completely damaged or lost.

Backup is one of the oldest terminologies to be heard, and it has gone through many evolutions. Nowadays, there are many vendors offering backup solutions.

In 2014, Microsoft announced that it will support backup as a service on its cloud (Azure), as a part of Azure Recovery Services, and since then, Azure Backup has undergone many enhancements.

Simply put, backing up your data to the cloud is currently one of the safest methods because of the ransomware attacks that have affected many organizations around the world.

Azure Backup has two kinds of vaults:

- **Backup vaults**: The older of the two, they have been widely used in the classic portal
- **Recovery Services vault**: The evolution of Backup vaults, they are designed to support Resource Manager deployments

> Backup vaults cannot be used to protect Resource Manager-based solutions. On the other hand, Recovery Services vaults can be used to protect classic deployments.

Azure Backup can protect data at different levels, either from the cloud or from your data center using different tools, as follows:

- **Azure Backup (Microsoft Azure Recovery Services (MARS)) agent**: This agent is responsible for backing up files and folders on Windows-based VMs. Also, it exists by default as an extension on Azure VMs, which are available in the Marketplace. However, that does not deny the fact that you can install it on VMs uploaded to Azure.
- **Azure Backup Server**: Is a **System Center Data Protection Manager (SCDPM)** on Azure, and it works with all SCDPM functionalities, except disk to tape backup. However, Azure Backup Server integration with System Center Products is not supported at the moment. It is used to back up application workloads, such as Hyper-V VMs, VMware VMs, SharePoint Server, Exchange server, SQL Server, and even **Bare Metal Recovery (BMR)**.
- **Azure VMs Backup**: Azure VMs Backup is designed for VM-level backup, as it backs up the whole VM using a backup extension.

Why Azure Backup?

Azure Backup delivers many key benefits to many environments that use it as a backup solution. Here are some of them:

- **Highly available and scalable solution**: When using Azure Backup, you do not have to care about the underlying infrastructure on which the backup will be stored, or the maintenance of that infrastructure. Also, whenever you need to back up and keep your data on Azure, you do not have to care about the size of the backed up data, because no matter what the size is, Azure will handle it.

- **Self-service**: Azure Backup will allocate your backed up data automatically without the need to assign it to a specific storage device.

- **High level of application consistency**: Azure Backup supports backing up Hyper-V, VMware VMs, SQL Servers, file servers, and so on. Whenever you restore any of these applications, you will not have to do any troubleshooting or fixing of the restored data, therefore, you can have your application up and running shortly after restoration.

- **Multiple storage replication types**: As covered in `Chapter 1`, *Understanding Azure Storage 101*, storage has many replication types, which are also supported for the storage on which the backed up data will be stored:
  - **Locally redundant storage (LRS)**: This option will replicate the backed up data three times to other storage devices within the same data center
  - **Geo-redundant storage (GRS)**: This option will replicate the backed up data to another data center in another region

- **Higher level of security**: For a higher level of security, Azure provides data encryption for the transmission of data to and from the cloud using an encryption passphrase. The encryption passphrase is stored locally, not on the cloud, and whenever you need to restore the data, you can use that passphrase.

- **Retain your data forever:** Traditionally, long-term backups were kept on tapes, but on Azure, you can keep your data as long as you wish.

The process of backing up data

Before backing up your data, you have to do some configuration, such as building a Recovery Services vault, which is the place where the backed up data will be stored. Once you have done that, you can start backing the data up.

Building a Recovery Services vault

As mentioned earlier, you have to build a Recovery Services vault to store your backed up data in. To do so, perform the following steps:

1. Navigate to **Recovery Services vaults**, as shown in the following screenshot:

Figure 6.1: Searching for Recovery Services vaults

2. Once the **Recovery Services vaults** blade is opened, you can create a new Recovery Services vault by clicking on **Add**, or **Create Recovery Services vaults**, as shown in the following screenshot:

Figure 6.2: Overview of Recovery Services vaults

3. Once you have clicked on **Add** or **Create Recovery Services vaults**, a new blade will pop up asking for a name for the vault, the subscription to which it will be assigned, the resource group on which it will exist, and the location it will be built on, as shown in the following screenshot:

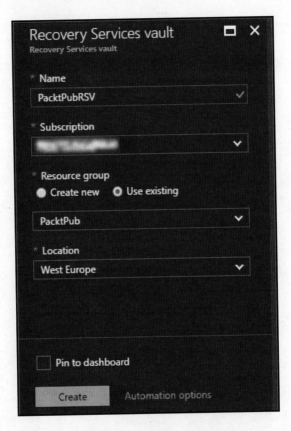

Figure 6.3: Creating a new Recovery Services vault

4. Click on **Create** and it will start the creation process of the Recovery Services vault, and within a few seconds, it will be built.

Backing up an Azure VM

Now, you have a Recovery Services vault to store and secure your backed up data in. The next step is to back something up, and in this section, we will back up an Azure VM:

1. Navigate to the Recovery Services vault you created, as shown in the following screenshot:

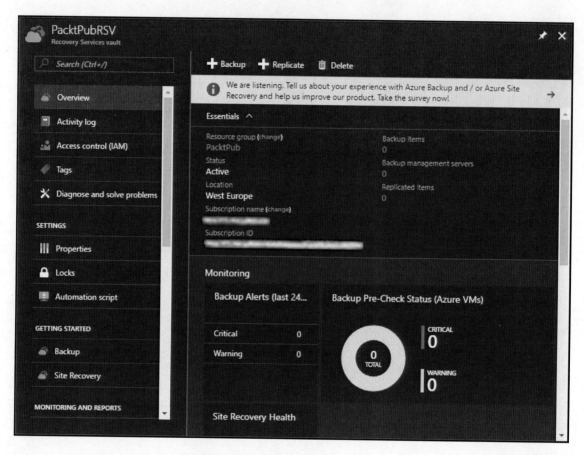

Figure 6.4: PacktPubSRV Recovery Services vault overview

2. To start the backup process, you can click on the **Backup** button on the console, or navigate to **Backup** under **GETTING STARTED** in the navigation pane, as shown in the following screenshot:

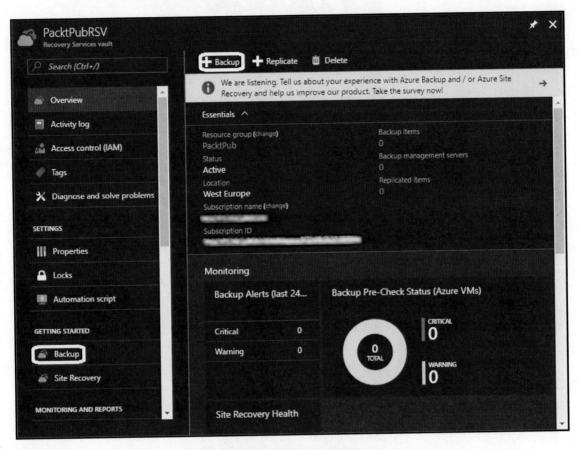

Figure 6.5: How to back up from the Recovery Services vault

3. Once you have clicked on **Backup**, a new blade will pop up asking about the following:
    - **Where is your workload running?** You have only two options: **Azure** or **On-Premises**
    - **What do you want to backup?** This depends on the answer to the previous question

If your workload is running on Azure, you will only have **Virtual machine** as a choice, as shown in the following screenshot:

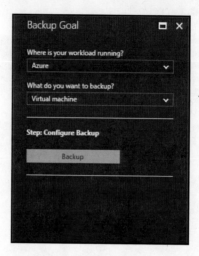

Figure 6.6: Backup options for workloads running on Azure

If your workload is running **On-Premises**, you can choose one or more of the following: **Files and folders**, **Hyper-V Virtual Machines**, **VMware Virtual Machines**, **Microsoft SQL Server**, **Microsoft SharePoint**, **Microsoft Exchange**, **System State**, and **Bare Metal Recovery** as shown in the following screenshot:

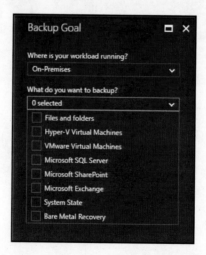

Figure 6.7: Backup options for workloads running on-premises

4. Since our workload is a **Virtual machine** running on Azure, I think you know which options we will select, and once they have been selected, we will click on **Backup**, as shown in the following screenshot:

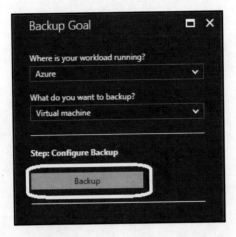

Figure 6.8: Configuring backup for Azure VM

5. Once you have clicked on **Backup**, a new blade will pop up where you can specify your backup policy, which includes: **BACKUP FREQUENCY** and **RETENTION RANGE**, as shown in the following screenshot:

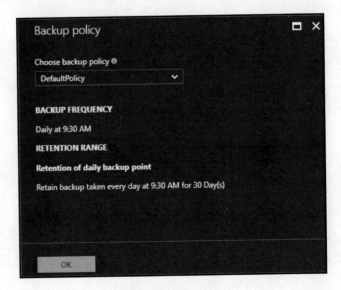

Figure 6.9: Backup default policy

6. The policy shown in the previous screenshot is a default policy that takes a backup daily at 9:30 a.m. and retains it for 30 days, but we need to create a backup policy that takes a backup on a weekly basis and retains the data for two weeks. As such, a new backup policy will be created, as shown in the following screenshot:

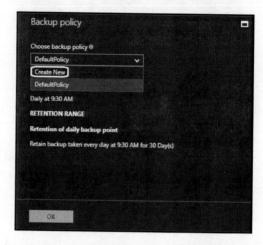

Figure 6.10: Choose to create a new backup policy

7. Once you have clicked on **Create New**, you will have to specify the **Policy name**, **Backup frequency**, and **Retention range**, as shown in the following screenshot:

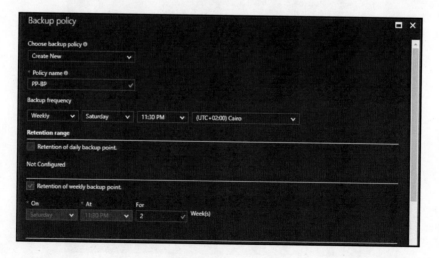

Figure 6.11: Configuring the new backup policy

8. By default, there will be a monthly and yearly backup point created with the specification, shown in the following screenshot. However, you can disable it by unmarking them:

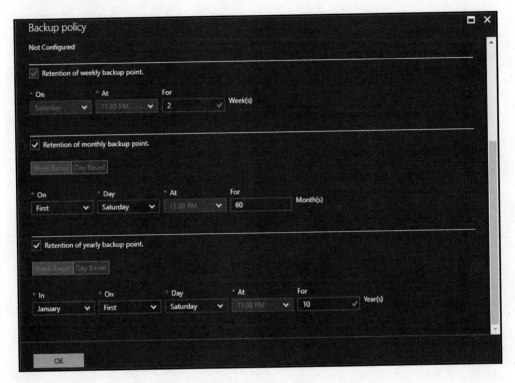

Figure 6.12: Monthly and yearly backup

9. Once you are done with your configurations, click **OK**.

10. Once you have clicked on **OK**, you will be navigated to a new blade in which you have to specify the virtual machine you need to back up, as shown in the following screenshot:

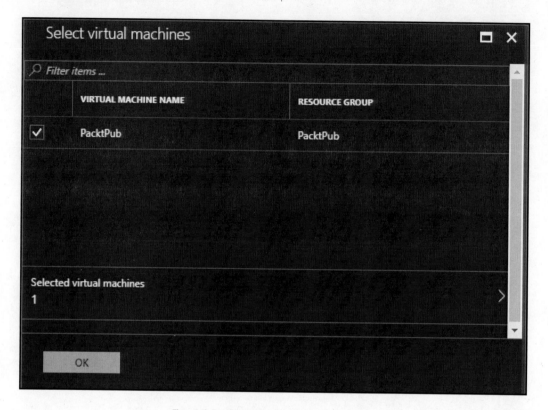

Figure 6.13: Specifying the virtual machine you want to back up

11. Once again, click on **OK**, and you will be navigated to a new blade where you have to enable backup, as shown in the following screenshot:

Figure 6.14: Enabling backup

12. Once the backup is enabled, the deployment will be kicked off, as shown in the following screenshot:

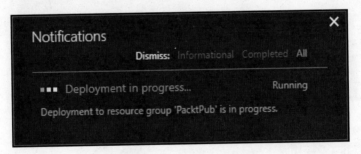

Figure 6.15: Deploying Azure Backup

13. Now, you are good to go and restore your data in the event of any data loss or corruption.

Restoring Azure VM files

A common situation that you might face is when you accidentally remove data or suffer a ransomware attack that encrypts your data. However, when you have your data backed up on Azure, you can be sure that you are on the right side. You will be able to recover your files and folders very easily just by taking the following steps:

1. Navigate to the affected VM for which you need to recover data. Under **OPERATIONS**, click on **Backup**, then **File Recovery**, as shown in the following screenshot:

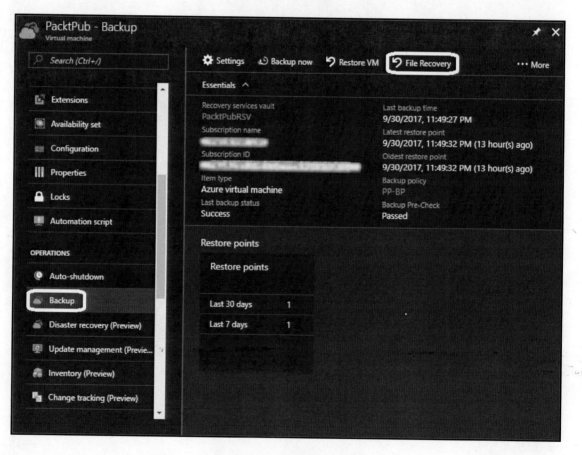

Figure 6.16: Recovering files for an Azure VM

2. Once you have clicked on **File Recovery**, a new blade will pop up where you have to select the recovery point to which you will be reverted to, as shown in the following screenshot:

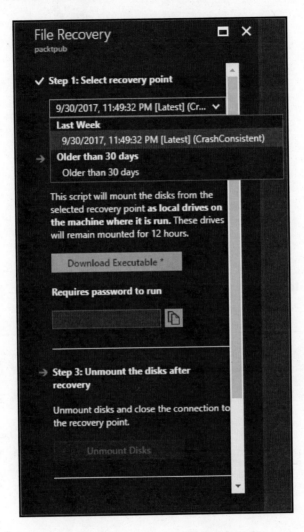

Figure 6.17: Selecting the recovery point you need to restore data from

3. Then, you have to download the executable, which is PowerShell-based and will require a password, as shown in the following screenshot:

Figure 6.18: Downloading the executable

4. Once the executable is downloaded, you have to run it in elevated mode (**Run as Administrator**), and enter the password that will run the script, as shown in the following screenshot:

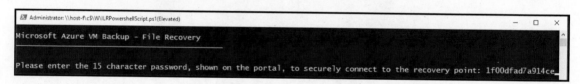

Figure 6.19: Running the executable

5. Then, it initiates a connection between the local machine and the recovery point. After that, it mounts the disks of the VM at that recovery point to the local machine to restore the files you need, as shown in the following screenshot:

```
Connecting to recovery point using ISCSI service....

Connection succeeded!

Please wait while we attach volumes of the recovery point.

1 recovery volumes attached

E:\Local Disk

*************  Open Explorer to browse for files  *************

After recovery, to remove the disks and close the connection to the recovery point, please click 'Unmount Disks' in step
  3 of the portal.

Press 'Q/q' key to exit ...
```

Figure 6.20: Connecting to the recovery point

6. Once you are done with restoring your lost and/or corrupted data, you can close the connection by unmounting disks from the VM, as shown in the following screenshot:

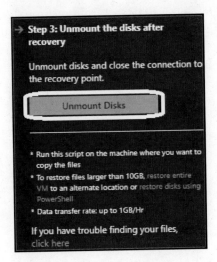

Figure 6.21: Unmounting disks from the VM

7. By now, you should have retrieved your lost data locally and be working on uploading it to Azure VM, or running the executable on the affected Azure VM itself and copying the data from the mounted disk to it--that would be a better solution for organizations with a slow internet connection.

Restoring Azure VM files key points

The following key points must be considered before restoring the VM files in order for the recovery process to go smoothly:

- Make sure that your firewall allows access to the following:
    - Outbound port 3260
    - microsoft.com
    - Azure endpoints used for Azure VM backups
- Start the Microsoft iSCSI Initiator service.
- The executable can only run successfully on an equivalent server OS or compatible client OS. For example, if your backed up VM is Windows Server 2016, you can run the executable on a Windows Server 2016 machine or Windows 10 machine.
- The mounted volume letter to your local machine does not have to match the volume letter on the Azure VM. It will assign the available letter to the mounted disk.
- The executable cannot be run on the affected VM in the following cases:
    - If the volumes are spanned and/or stripped
    - If the disks are mirrored or in RAID5

 If you face any issues during the recovery process after implementing the previously mentioned key points, you can check out the following URL: https://docs.microsoft.com/en-us/azure/backup/backup-azure-restore-files-from-vm#troubleshooting.

Restoring an Azure VM

Your VM might have viruses or have some applications that malfunction. In such cases, you might consider restoring the VM itself to a previous recovery point, and to do so, you have to perform the following steps:

1. Navigate to the affected VM that needs to be recovered. Under **OPERATIONS**, click on **Backup**, then **Restore VM**, as shown in the following screenshot:

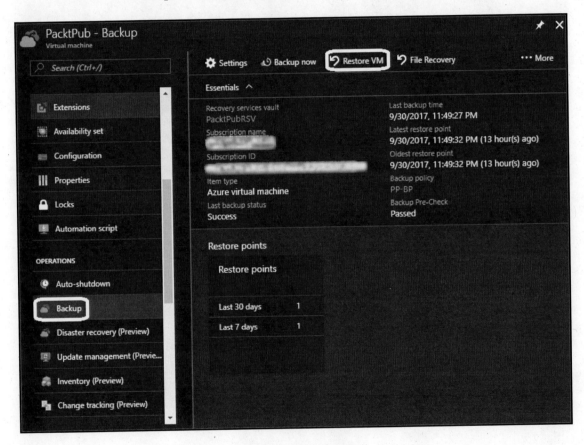

Figure 6.22: Restoring an Azure VM

2. Once you have clicked on **Restore VM**, a new blade will be opened where you have to specify to which restore point you want to revert, as shown in the following screenshot:

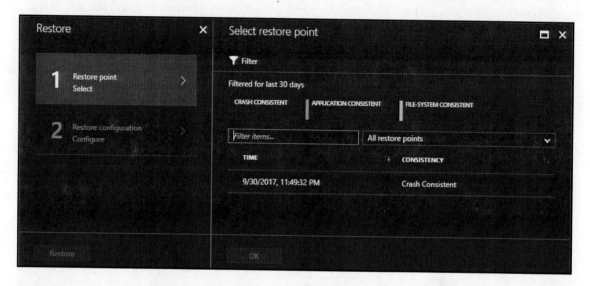

Figure 6.23: Selecting the restore point

3. Once the restore point is selected, you will be navigated to another blade where you will have to specify the following configuration:
   - **Restore Type**: There are two types of restoration: **Create virtual machine** and **Restore disks**, and as the name implies, the first one will create a new virtual machine with the storage and configuration of the VM at the time the restore point was taken in
   - **Virtual machine name**: If **Create virtual machine** is selected, you will be asked to specify its name
   - **Resource group**: The resource group in which the VM will reside
   - **Virtual network**: The virtual network to which the VM will belong
   - **Subnet**: The subnet from which the VM will acquire an IP

- **Storage Account**: This field exists for both restore types, and you have to specify a storage account to which the disks will be restored:

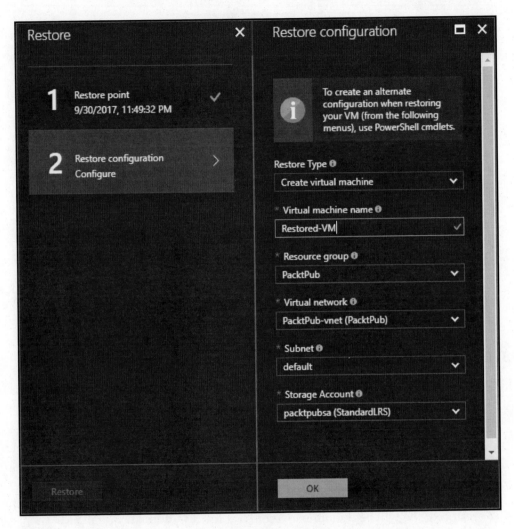

Figure 6.24: Specify the restore configuration

4. Once you have clicked on **OK**, you are good to go by clicking on **Restore point**, as shown in the following screenshot:

Figure 6.25: Restoring the VM

5. Once the restoration is done, you can navigate to **Virtual machines** and check the restored VM.

Restoring an Azure VM key points

The following key points must be considered before restoring a VM in order for the recovery process to go smoothly:

- If you are restoring a VM with managed disks, you should disable **Storage service encryption** for the storage account to which the disks will be restored.
- It is recommended to reinstall the extensions that were added to the VM before the backup.
- If you have set a static public IP for the VM before backup, the public IP for the restored VM will be dynamic to avoid a conflict with the original VM.
- If you want to add the restored VM to an availability set, you have to restore the disks first, then create a VM and attach the disks to it. You will be able to add the VM to an availability set during VM creation, but cannot do so during the restoration process.

Further information

For further information about Azure Backup, you can check out the following links:

- **Configure an offline backup**: https://docs.microsoft.com/en-us/azure/backup/backup-azure-backup-import-export
- **Prepare Azure Backup Server**: https://docs.microsoft.com/en-us/azure/backup/backup-azure-microsoft-azure-backup
- **Add storage to Azure Backup Server**: https://docs.microsoft.com/en-us/azure/backup/backup-mabs-add-storage
- **Backup VMware Server using Azure Backup**: https://docs.microsoft.com/en-us/azure/backup/backup-azure-backup-server-vmware
- **Backup Exchange Server using Azure Backup**: https://docs.microsoft.com/en-us/azure/backup/backup-azure-exchange-mabs
- **Backup SharePoint Server using Azure Backup**: https://docs.microsoft.com/en-us/azure/backup/backup-azure-backup-sharepoint-mabs
- **Backup SQL Server using Azure Backup**: https://docs.microsoft.com/en-us/azure/backup/backup-azure-sql-mabs
- **Protect system state and BMR**: https://docs.microsoft.com/en-us/azure/backup/backup-mabs-system-state-and-bmr
- **Recover data from Azure Backup Server**: https://docs.microsoft.com/en-us/azure/backup/backup-azure-alternate-dpm-server
- **Application consistent backup of Azure Linux VMs (preview)**: https://docs.microsoft.com/en-us/azure/backup/backup-azure-linux-app-consistent
- **Configure backup reports**: https://docs.microsoft.com/en-us/azure/backup/backup-azure-configure-reports

Automating tasks

So, we have reached the final destination of the chapter, where we automate all of the manual tasks that we have covered.

Building a Recovery Services vault using Azure PowerShell

To work with Azure Recovery Services, you have to register the Recovery Services provider by running the following cmdlet:

```
Register-AzureRmResourceProvider -ProviderNamespace
"Microsoft.RecoveryServices"
```

Then, you can create the Recovery Services vault by running the following cmdlet:

```
New-AzureRmRecoveryServicesVault -Name PSRS -ResourceGroupName "PacktPub" -
Location "West Europe"
```

Building a Recovery Services vault using the Azure CLI 2.0

In order to run Azure Backup commands using the Azure CLI 2.0, you have to upgrade to the latest version of the Azure CLI 2.0 from the following link: `https://azurecliprod.` `blob.core.windows.net/msi/azure-cli-2.0.18.msi`.

Once downloaded and installed, you can run the following command to create a Recovery Services vault:

```
az backup vault create --resource-group PacktPub --name CLIRS --location
westeurope
```

Backing up an Azure VM using Azure PowerShell

First off, you have to set the vault context to apply it to all subsequent cmdlets by running the following cmdlet:

```
Get-AzureRmRecoveryServicesVault -Name PSRS | Set-
AzureRmRecoveryServicesVaultContext
```

At the time of writing, you cannot change the backup frequency using PowerShell. However, you can change the retention using the following cmdlets. Considering that, I will put the result in a variable, as it will be used later:

```
$SchedulePolicy = Get-AzureRmRecoveryServicesBackupSchedulePolicyObject -
WorkloadType "AzureVM"
$RetentionPolicy = Get-AzureRmRecoveryServicesBackupRetentionPolicyObject -
```

```
WorkloadType "AzureVM"
$RetentionPolicy.DailySchedule.DurationCountInDays = 14
```

Now, you can build your own backup policy by running the following cmdlet:

```
New-AzureRmRecoveryServicesBackupProtectionPolicy -Name PSBPolicy -
WorkloadType "AzureVM" -RetentionPolicy $RetentionPolicy -SchedulePolicy
$SchedulePolicy
```

Finally, you have a policy that you can assign to Azure VMs. Therefore, we will put the policy in a variable, then assign it to an Azure VM by running the following cmdlets:

```
$Policy=Get-AzureRmRecoveryServicesBackupProtectionPolicy -Name PSBPolicy
Enable-AzureRmRecoveryServicesBackupProtection -Policy $Policy -Name
PacktPubVM -ResourceGroupName PacktPub
```

 The time zone of the time shown in PowerShell is UTC. Take into consideration that the one shown in the portal matches your local system clock.

Backing up an Azure VM using the Azure CLI 2.0

First off, you have to create a backup policy, which can be done by creating a JSON encoded policy definition and passing it to the Azure CLI, as you will see shortly, or by using the default policy.

To create a new backup policy, run the following command:

```
az backup policy set -policy <JSON encoded policy definition> -- resource-
group PacktPub -vault-name CLIRS
```

Or, to use the default backup policy, you can run the following command:

```
az backup policy get-default-for-vm --resource-group PacktPub --vault-name
CLIRS
```

Then, you can start the backup process by running the following command:

```
az backup protection enable-for-vm --policy-name get-default-for-vm --
resource-group PacktPub --vault-name CLIRS --vm PacktPubVM
```

Restoring Azure VM files using Azure PowerShell

At the time of writing, you cannot carry out the file recovery process completely using PowerShell. You have to do one part through the portal, and the other part using the executable PowerShell script, as shown earlier.

Restoring Azure VM files using the Azure CLI 2.0

To do so, we will have to specify the Recovery Services vault and the container within which the recovery points exist, and if you want to retrieve the name of the vaults and the container names, you can run the following commands:

```
az backup vault list --resource-group PacktPub
az backup container list --resource-group PacktPub --vault-name CLIRS
```

Then, you can run the following command, which will download the executable PowerShell script that will be run to mount the disks to the local machine you are running the script from:

```
az backup restore files mount-rp --resource-group PacktPub --vault-name
CLIRS --container-name <The name of the container within which the recovery
points are stored>--item-name <The name of the backedup item> --rp-name
<The name of the recovery point>
```

Restoring an Azure VM using Azure PowerShell

Unlike the recovery process to the Azure VM via the portal we went through earlier, Azure PowerShell can only restore disks. You can then create a new VM from the restored disks, which means you cannot restore the VM directly, as we did earlier.

Since the backed up items are stored in containers, we have to retrieve the container name first by running the following cmdlet:

```
$Container = Get-AzureRmRecoveryServicesBackupContainer  -ContainerType
"AzureVM" -Status "Registered" -FriendlyName "PacktPub"
```

Then, we have to specify the backup item that specifies the workload type by running the following cmdlet:

```
$BackupItem = Get-AzureRmRecoveryServicesBackupItem -Container $Container
-WorkloadType "AzureVM"
```

After that, we have to specify the period within which we need to restore data by specifying the start and end date, which will be within the last five days:

```
$SD = (Get-Date).AddDays(-5)
$ED = Get-Date
```

Now, we can retrieve all the recovery points within this period by running the following cmdlet:

```
$RecoveryPoint = Get-AzureRmRecoveryServicesBackupRecoveryPoint -Item
$BackupItem -StartDate $SD.ToUniversalTime() -EndDate $ED.ToUniversalTime()
```

If there are multiple recovery points within this period and you want to restore a specific recovery point, you can retrieve it by its index, and since there is only one recovery point, we can retrieve it by running the following cmdlet:

```
$RecoveryPoint[0]
```

Finally, you can restore the backed up disks by running the following cmdlet:

```
Restore-AzureRmRecoveryServicesBackupItem -RecoveryPoint $RecoveryPoint[0]
-StorageAccountName "Specify the destination Storage Account to which the
disks will be restored to" -StorageAccountResourceGroupName "Speciify the
resource group within which the storage account exists"
```

Using what you have learned throughout the previous chapter, you can create a new VM with the restored disks attached to it.

Restoring an Azure VM using the Azure CLI 2.0

As with the restoration process using PowerShell, we cannot restore the VM to being up and running, therefore we will restore the disks by running the following command:

```
az backup restore restore-disks --container-name <The name of the
container> --item-name <The name of the backedup item> --resource-group
PacktPub --rp-name <The name of the recovery point> --storage-account <The
name or ID of the storage account to which the disks will be restored> --
vault-name <The name of the recovery services vault>
```

Then, you can create a VM with the restored disks attached to it.

Summary

We are done with the first part of Azure Recovery Services. Throughout the chapter, we have covered the importance of Azure Backup, how to use it and even how to use it to back up your data.

The next chapter will cover the other part of Azure Recovery Services. Azure Site Recovery is one of the most important services that Azure provides for the business continuity, and it will be covered in detail in the coming chapter.

7
Azure Site Recovery

In this chapter, **Azure Site Recovery** (**ASR**) will be introduced as a business continuity solution. We'll look at why it should be used and which environments it supports. Then, the prerequisites for preparing an environment will be covered, followed by how to enable replication and create recovery plans. After that, you will learn how to check whether ASR is functioning properly or not. Finally, links to more information about ASR will be provided for you to gain more knowledge about it.

The following topics will be covered:

- Introduction to ASR
- ASR supportability
- Preparing your environment for ASR
- Kicking off replication from on-premises to ASR
- ASR recovery plans
- Testing ASR
- Further information

Introduction to ASR

Business continuity is one of the most important key points, especially for enterprises. Building a disaster recovery site is a must-do step to take in order to have an optimal environment. That is why Microsoft Azure provides ASR services, which can be used to build your disaster recovery site.

This service helps to ensure that your applications are up and running all the time, even if a disaster happens to your data center.

When using ASR, you can build your own disaster recovery site for your Azure VMs, your on-premises VMs and/or physical servers, or even manage replication between a primary and secondary site.

In March 2015, Microsoft announced the launch of ASR and, since then, this service has undergone many enhancements and added features according to the customers' feedback.

ASR supportability

At the time of writing, ASR supports replication from the following sources:

- Hyper-V Server 2012 R2 and 2016
- vSphere 5.5, 6.0, and 6.5
- Physical servers

Hyper-V servers

As mentioned earlier, you can only replicate Hyper-V VMs from Windows Server 2012 R2 and Windows Server 2016. However, if you are managing your Hyper-V hosts with **System Center Virtual Machine Manager** (**SCVMM**), you can use it to replicate VMs from Hyper-V hosts.

At the time of writing, SCVMM 2012 R2 and 2016 are the supported versions to work with ASR.

 You need to install the latest updates for your Hyper-V hosts and SCVMM to avoid any issues during replication. Also, you need to make sure that your SCVMM 2016 cloud does not support the co-existence of Windows Server 2016 and Windows Server 2012 R2 hosts. If there are any configurations that include the upgrade from SCVMM 2012 R2 to 2016, it will not be supported.

The following table specifies the supported and unsupported configurations for Hyper-V hosts and guests during replication:

	Supported	Unsupported
Guest OSes	You can check the following link to see the supported OSes: `https://technet. microsoft.com/library/ cc794868.aspx`	Any OS that is not mentioned on the previous link is not supported
Hyper-V network configurations	• NIC Teaming • VLANS • IPv4	IPv6
Guest network configurations	• IPv4 • Static IP address for Windows-based VMs • Multiple NICs for the same VM	• IPv6 • NIC Teaming • Static IP addresses for Linux-based VMs
Azure network configuration for Hyper-V guests	• Express route • Internal and external load balancers • Traffic manager • Multiple NICs • IPv4 • Reserved IPs • You can retain your source IP addresses	None
Hyper-V host storage configurations	• SMB 3.0 • SAN (iSCSI) • **Multipath I/O (MPIO)**	None

Hyper-V guest storage configurations	• VHD and VHDX • Generation 2 VMs • EFI and UEFI • Maximum disk space is 4059 GB • Disk with the 4k sector is supported for generation 1 VMs • You can have a volume with a striped disk with a size of more than 1 TB for Windows-based VMs • LVM logical volume management is supported for Linux-based VMs • Storage spaces • Disk exclusion • MPIO	• SMB 3.0 • Shared cluster disk • Encrypted disk • Disks with 4k sector size are not supported for generation 2 VMs • Hot add and remove for disks
Azure Storage configurations for Hyper-V guests	• LRS, GRS, and RA-GRS • Premium Storage • Encryption at rest (**Storage Service Encryption** (**SSE**))	• Cool and hot storage • Azure import/export service
Azure compute configurations for Hyper-V guests	• Availability sets service • **Hybrid User Benefit** (**HUB**) • Managed disks service	Managed disks service is not supported when failing back to on-premises

VMware vSphere and physical servers

As mentioned earlier, you can use Azure as a DR site for your VMware vSphere and physical servers. However, you have to ensure that the versions of VMware vSphere are 5.5, 6.0, or 6.5, and the same goes for vCenter if you want to replicate from it.

	Supported	Unsupported
VMware guest machines and physical server OSes	The following Windows-based OSes: • Windows Server 2008 R2 SP1 • Windows Server 2012 • Windows Server 2012 R2 The following Linux-based OSes: • **Red Hat**: 5.2 to 5.11, 6.1 to 6.9, 7.0 to 7.3 • **CentOS**: 5.2 to 5.11, 6.1 to 6.9, 7.0 to 7.3 • Debian 7, 8 • SUSE Linux Enterprise Server 11 SP3, SP4 • Ubuntu 14.04, 16.04 LTS server for the kernel version URLs that can be checked from the following link: `https://docs.microsoft.com/en-us/azure/site-recovery/site-recovery-support-matrix-to-azure#supported-ubuntu-kernel-versions-for-vmwarephysical-servers` • Oracle Enterprise Linux 6.4, 6.5 which run either a Red Hat compatible kernel or Unbreakable Enterprise Kernel Release 3	Other OSes are not supported
VMware hosts/physical server network configurations	• NIC Teaming is supported for VMware • VLANs • IPv4	• IPv6 • NIC Teaming is not supported for physical servers

VMware guests/physical servers network configurations	• IPv4 • Static IP addresses for Windows-based and Linux-based VMs • Using multiple NICs for the same VM	• IPv6 • NIC Teaming
Azure network configurations for VMware guests/physical servers	• Express route • Internal and external load balancers • Traffic manager • Multiple NICs • IPv4 • Reserved IPs • You can retain your source IP addresses	None
VMware hosts/physical servers storage configurations	• NFS is supported for VMware hosts • SAN (iSCSI) • MPIO	NFS is not supported for physical servers.
VMware guests/physical servers storage configurations	• VMDK • RDM is supported for VMware hosts • Maximum disk space is 4059 GB • Disk with 4k sector is supported • You can have a volume with striped disk with a size of more than 1 TB for Windows-based VMs • **Logical Volume Management (LVM)** is supported for Linux based VMs • Disk exclusion	• SMB 3.0 • Shared cluster disk • Encrypted disk • Hot add and remove for disks • EFI and UEFI • NFS • Storage spaces
Azure Storage configurations for VMware guests/physical servers	• LRS, GRS, and RA-GRS • Premium Storage • Encryption at rest (SSE)	• Cool and hot storage • Azure Import/Export service
Azure compute configurations for VMware guests/physical servers	• Availability sets service • HUB • Managed disks service	None

If you have a SUSE Linux Enterprise Server 11 SP3 on-premises, and you have updated it to SP4, replication will fail, as this is not a supported scenario at the time of writing. In order to do so, you have to disable replication until you update it, then you can enable replication again once you are done with the update.

The following Windows-based OS is not supported:

- Windows Server 2016

So far, you should be aware of what is and isn't supported to kick off replication to Azure. However, for more information, especially on advanced scenarios, you might be interested in reading about the following topics:

- Failed-over Azure VM requirements: `https://docs.microsoft.com/en-us/azure/site-recovery/site-recovery-support-matrix-to-azure#failed-over-azure-vm-requirements`
- Support for Recovery Services vault: `https://docs.microsoft.com/en-us/azure/site-recovery/site-recovery-support-matrix-to-azure#support-for-recovery-services-vault-actions`
- What workloads you can protect with ASR: `https://docs.microsoft.com/en-us/azure/site-recovery/site-recovery-workload`

Preparing your environment for ASR

Before starting the replication between your on-premises and Azure, the environment needs to be prepared by building a site-to-site VPN connection, then installing and registering the ASR provider.

Building a site-to-site VPN connection

In this topic, we will go through the process of building a site-to-site VPN connection, considering **Routing and Remote Access Service (RRAS)** as the local VPN.

You can have your local VPN device, such as Cisco, Juniper, Brocade, and so on. You can check the supported VPN devices list at the following link: `https://docs.microsoft.com/en-us/azure/vpn-gateway/vpn-gateway-about-vpn-devices`.

Without further ado, let's get started with the steps:

1. Create an on-premises VM or use a physical server to act as the local VPN gateway with two NICs. One for internal communication with an internal IP address assigned to it, but without a default gateway to make sure the traffic will be routed from the other NIC. The other one will be responsible for communicating with the Azure site with a public IP assigned to it with its default gateway.

Since IPv6 is not used in such a scenario, you can disable IPv6 for both NICs. Also, you have to uncheck everything for the external NIC, except TCP/IPv4, and disable NetBIOS over TCP.

In order to disable NetBIOS over TCP, you have to navigate to TCP/IPv4 properties **Advanced | WINS | Disable NetBIOS over TCP/IP**.

2. Once the VM/physical server is up and running, you can install RRAS. We will select the **Direct Access and VPN (RAS)** role service.
3. Then, we will navigate to the Azure portal to create a virtual network, and to do so, we will navigate to the **Virtual networks** blade and click on **Add**, as shown in the following screenshot:

Figure 7.1: Virtual networks blade

4. Once you have clicked on **Add**, a new blade will pop up asking you to fill in the fields shown in the following screenshot and then click on **Create**:

Figure 7.2: Creating a virtual network

5. Once the virtual network is created, we will need to add a gateway subnet, which will be used for the virtual network gateway. To do so, navigate to the virtual network you created. You will find **Subnets** under **SETTINGS**, as shown in the following screenshot:

Figure 7.3: Azure virtual network subnets

6. Click on **Gateway subnet** and fill in the fields, as shown in the following screenshot:

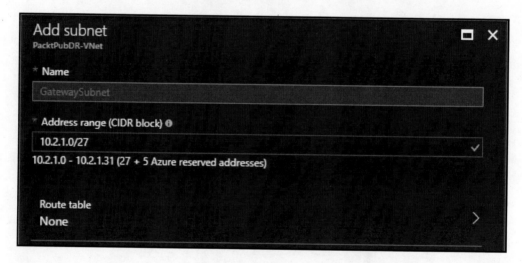

Figure 7.4: Adding a gateway subnet

7. Once you are done with adding the **Gateway subnet**, you can navigate to **More services** and search for `virtual network gateway`, as shown in the following screenshot:

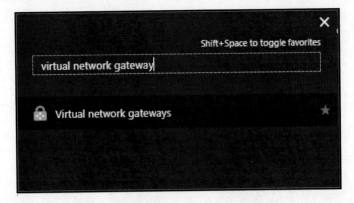

Figure 7.5: Searching for virtual network gateway services

8. Once the **Virtual network gateways** blade is opened, you can click on **Add** to add your virtual network gateway, as shown in the following screenshot:

Figure 7.6: Virtual network gateways blade

9. Once you have clicked on **Add**, you have to specify the following settings:
   - **Name**: The name of the virtual network gateway
   - **Gateway type**: In this scenario, **VPN** will be selected
   - **VPN type**: In this scenario, it will be **Route-based**
   - **SKU**: **VpnGw1** will be selected for our scenario
   - **Virtual network**: Select the virtual network within which the gateway subnet exists, and once it is selected, you will have to specify a public IP address
   - **Subscription**: Specify the subscription that is going to charge this service
   - **Location**: Specify which location the virtual network gateway will be built

For more information about gateway SKUs, you can check out the following link: `https://docs.microsoft.com/en-us/azure/vpn-gateway/vpn-gateway-about-vpngateways#gwsku`.

10. Once you have clicked on **Create**, the creation process will start and will take a while.

11. In the meanwhile, we can search for `local network gateways`, as shown in the following screenshot:

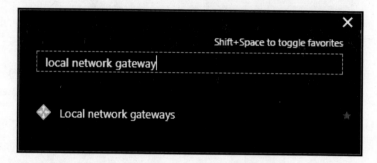

Figure 7.7: Searching for local network gateways

12. Click on **Local network gateways** and a new blade will pop up where you will have to click on **Add** to create a new local network gateway, as shown in the following screenshot:

Figure 7.8: Local network gateways blade

13. Once you have clicked on **Add**, the following fields need to be filled in:
    - **Name**: The name of the local network gateway
    - **IP address**: The public IP address of the RRAS server
    - **Address space**: Add the address space of your local network
    - **Subscription**: Specify which subscription is going to be charged for this service
    - **Resource group**: Specify which resource group will host the local network gateway
    - **Location**: The location in which this local network gateway is going to be built

14. Click on **Create** but do not proceed until the virtual network gateway and local network gateway are created.

15. Once the virtual network gateway and local network gateway are created, you can navigate to either of them and, under **SETTINGS**, click on **Connections**.

16. Click on **Add** to add a connection between the local network gateway and the virtual network gateway.

17. Once you have clicked on **Add**, a new blade will pop up, and you will have to fill in the following fields:
    - **Name**: The name of the connection
    - **Virtual network gateway**: Specify the virtual network gateway that was created earlier
    - **Shared key**: Specify a shared key, which will be used to initiate the connections from on-premises

18. Once the connection is created, open the **Routing and Remote Access** console on the RRAS Server, as shown in the following screenshot:

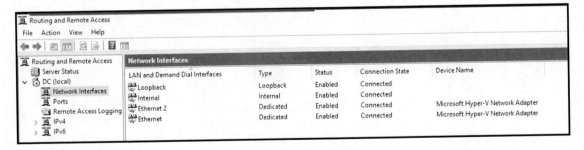

Figure 7.9: Routing and Remote Access console

19. Right-click on **Network interfaces** and select **New Demand-dial Interface**.
20. A welcome wizard will pop up. To proceed, click **Next**.
21. Name the interface.
22. Select the connection type, which will be **VPN** in this scenario.
23. Select the VPN type, which is **IKEv2** in this scenario.
24. Then, enter the public IP address of the virtual network gateway that was created earlier on Azure.
25. **Select transports and security options for this connection.** ; will be left as the default **Route IP packets on this interface**.
26. In this step, you have to specify the static route to the Azure virtual network that your on-premises VMs and physical servers will use when they are migrated to Azure. So, you can click on **Add** and set your Azure virtual network information, as shown in the following screenshot:

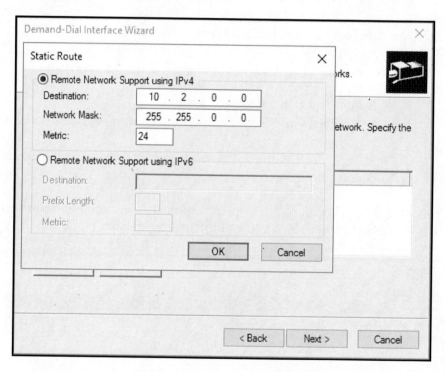

Figure 7.10: Setting the static route to the Azure virtual network

27. For the dial-out credentials, you can enter the username: `Azure`.

28. Once we are done with all steps, we can click on **Finish**.

29. The configurations are not yet done. Therefore, once the demand-dial interface is created, we will open its properties.

30. Navigate to the **Security** tab. Under **Authentication**, **User preshared key for authentication** will be selected, and the shared key that was entered earlier when creating the connection between the local network gateway and the virtual network gateway will be entered, as shown in the following screenshot:

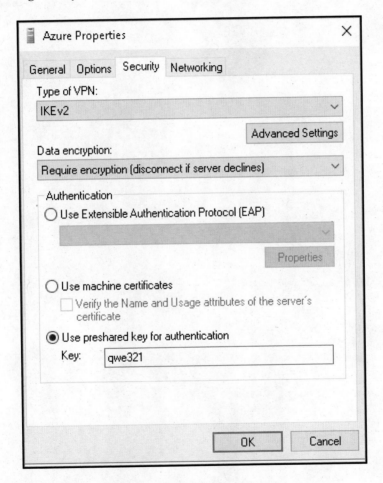

Figure 7.11: Setting the authentication type

31. Now, we can initiate the connection between on-premises and Azure by right-clicking on the interface and clicking on **Connect**.

Preparing an infrastructure for replication

Now, your on-premises can communicate with Azure Cloud. Therefore, let's go ahead and complete the preparation:

1. Navigate to the Azure portal again, and open the recovery services vault. Select the recovery services vault that was created in the previous chapter, and navigate to **Site Recovery**, as shown in the following screenshot:

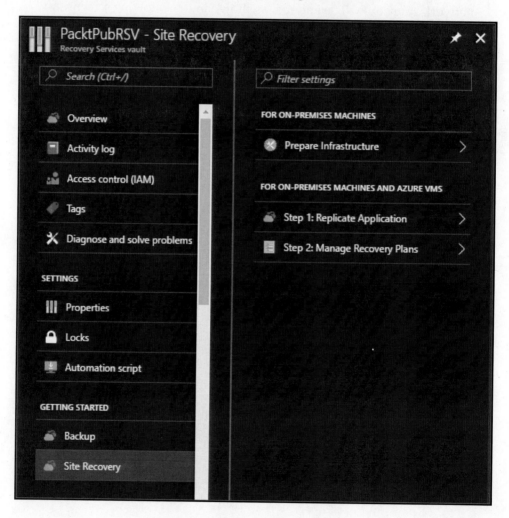

Figure 7.12: ASR blade

2. Click on **Prepare Infrastructure** and a new blade will pop up where you have to specify the location of the machines you want to replicate, and to where they will be replicated. But if the machines are on-premises, you have to specify whether the machines are virtualized or not, and if they are virtualized with Hyper-V, you have to specify whether they are managed with SCVMM or not, as shown in the following screenshot:

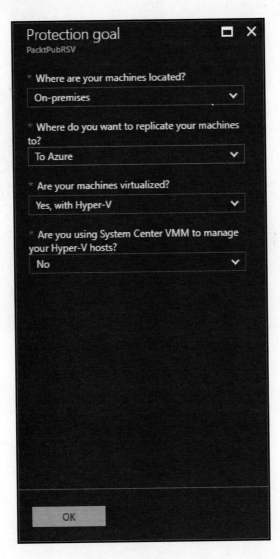

Figure 7.13: Specify the protection goal

3. Then, you have to prepare the source, where you have to specify a Hyper-V site if one exists, or create a new one, as shown in the following screenshot:

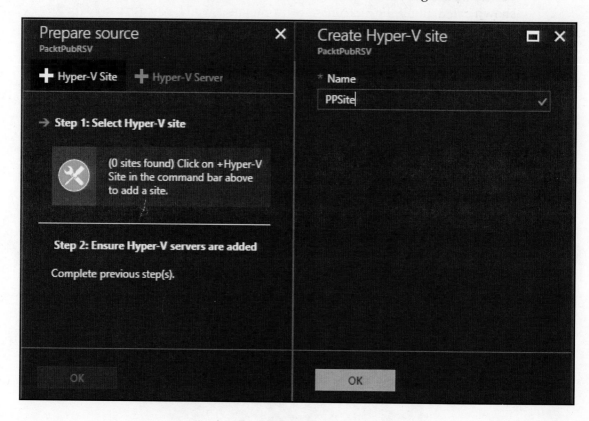

Figure 7.14: Creating a Hyper-V site

4. Once the site is created, click on **Hyper-V Server**, and a new blade will pop up to download the installer of the ASR provider and the vault registration key, as shown in the following screenshot:

Figure 7.15: Download the ASR provider and the vault registration key

If you have a proxy in your environment, you can click on **Service URLs** to check the required ports you need to open.

5. Once they are downloaded, install them on your Hyper-V host. To do so, run the installer, and the installation wizard will pop up, where you have to specify whether the Microsoft update will be allowed or not for ASR.

6. After that, you have to specify the installation location of the provider and click **Install**.

7. Once the installation is done, you can either register the vault registration key or finish the installation and register it later, but we will move on and register it.

8. To register the provider, you have to browse for the vault registration key downloaded earlier, and it will fill the other fields, as shown in the following screenshot:

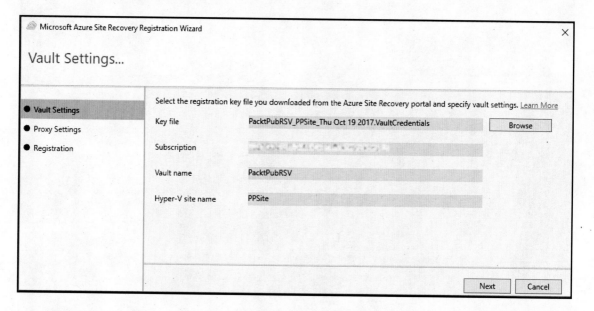

Figure 7.16: Importing the vault registration key

9. Then, you have to specify whether you will connect to ASR directly or via a proxy, as shown in the following screenshot:

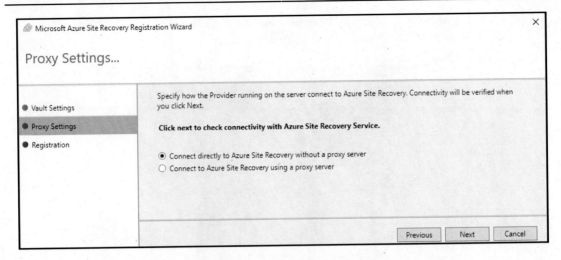

Figure 7.17: Specifying the proxy settings for the connection

10. Once it is connected to ASR, the host will register itself to the ASR vault, as shown in the following screenshot:

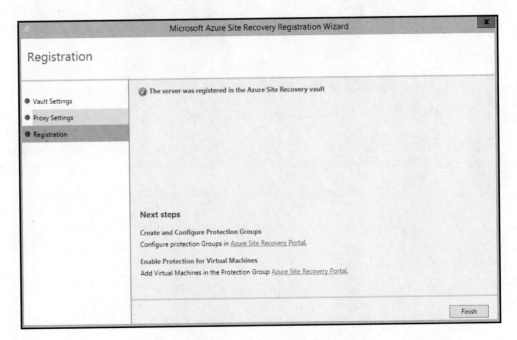

Figure 7.18: The host is successfully registered

11. After about 30 minutes, the host will be added to the site we created earlier on Azure, as shown in the following screenshot:

Figure 7.19: The Hyper-V server has been added

 You can refresh the portal and try again after a while if the server was not detected in the blade shown in the previous screenshot.

12. Then, you will be navigated to a new blade where you have to specify the subscription and the deployment model. It will also do some checks, as shown in the following screenshot:

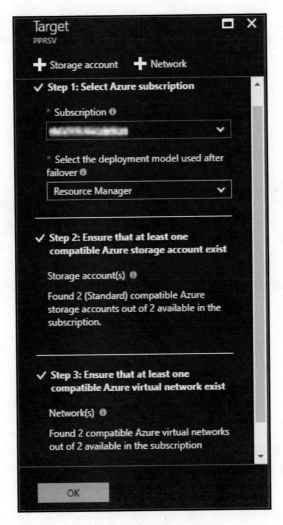

Figure 7.20: Specify target settings

13. After that, you will be navigated to a new blade where you have to specify a replication policy, and since we have not created any policies yet, we create and associate a policy, as shown in the following screenshot:

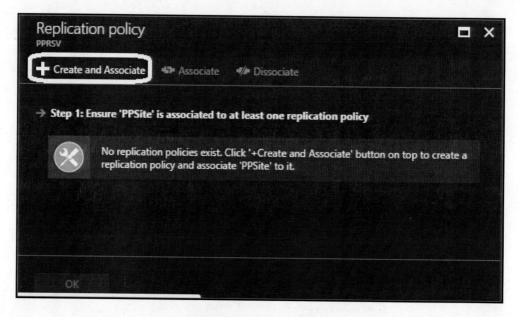

Figure 7.21: Create a replication policy

14. Once clicked on **Create and Associate**, you will have to specify the following settings:
    - **Name**: The name of the policy
    - **Copy frequency**: Specify how frequently data should be synchronized between source and target locations

- **Recovery point retention in hours**: Number of hours up to which the recovery points will be retained
- **App-consistent snapshot frequency in hours**: Frequency at which an application consistent snapshot is taken for the VMs
- **Initial replication start time**: The time at which the initial replication will be kicked off

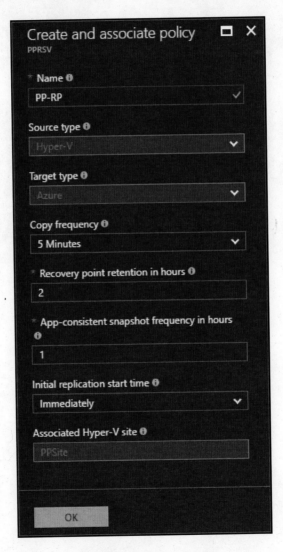

Figure 7.22: Specify replication policy settings

15. Once you have clicked on **OK**, you have to wait until the replication policy is created and associated, as shown in the following screenshot:

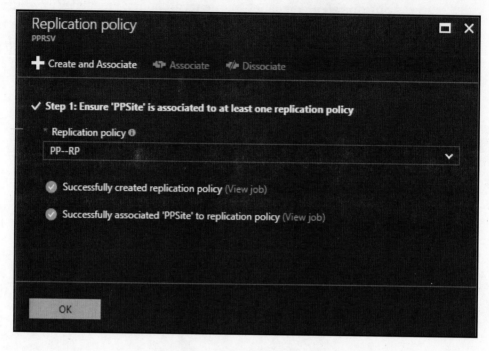

Figure 7.23: Creating and associating the replication policy

16. The last step in preparing your infrastructure for ASR is whether you are you done with the **Deployment planning**, as shown in the following screenshot:

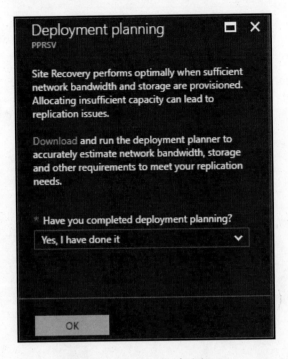

Figure 7.24: Specify your readiness for deployment

17. Now you are done with all the required prerequisites for ASR replication.

Kicking off replication from on-premises to ASR

By now, we are good to go ahead and start our replication by following these steps:

1. Since we are done with preparing the infrastructure, we can go ahead to step 1 of Azure replication, as shown in the following screenshot:

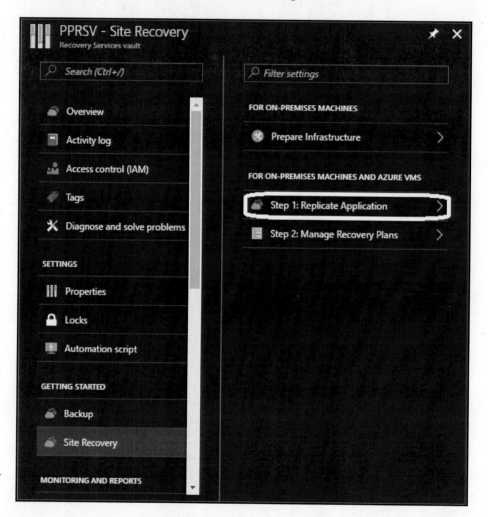

Figure 7.25: Step 1 of Azure replication

2. Then, you have to specify the source and its location, as shown in the following screenshot:

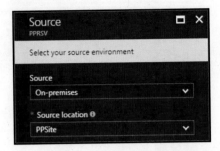

Figure 7.26: Specify the replication source

3. After that, you have to specify some settings for the target, as shown in the following screenshot:

Figure 7.27: Specify the target settings

4. Now, you can specify which VMs you want to be replicated to ASR, as shown in the following screenshot:

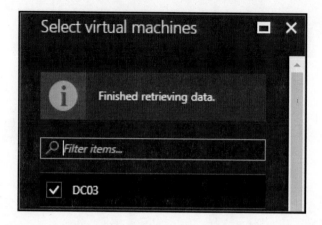

Figure 7.28: Select the VMs you want to be replicated

5. Once the VM is selected, you have to specify the OS type, as shown in the following screenshot:

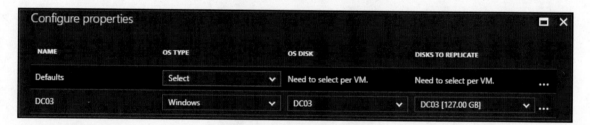

Figure 7.29: The VM properties

6. Finally, you have to select the replication policy you want to assign to it, as shown in the following screenshot:

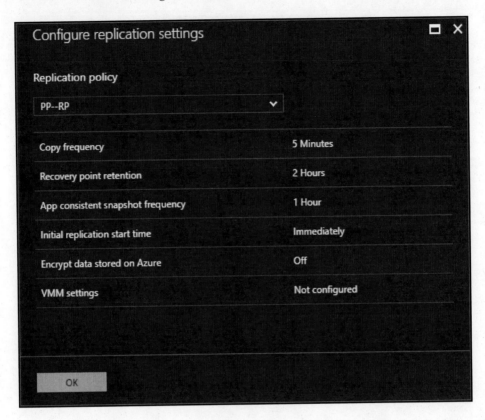

Figure 7.30: Select the replication policy

7. Now, you only have to click on **Enable replication**, and the replication will be kicked off, as shown in the following screenshot:

Figure 7.31: Enable the replication

ASR recovery plans

It is not common to have ASR without a recovery plan, especially for large environments where you have domain controllers, web servers, SQL Servers, SharePoint Servers, Exchange Servers, and so on.

If there is no recovery plan when failover of the servers to Azure takes place, they will start randomly, and that will affect many machines. For example, if the SharePoint Server starts first without the domain controller and SQL Server up and running, that will cause issues. Therefore, you need to make a recovery plan to specify the dependencies of the machines.

The recovery plan would do the following:

- Specify the machines that would failover together and failback together
- Specify the dependencies between machines so that machines with higher priorities, such as domain controllers, start first.

To create a recovery plan, you have to follow these steps:

1. Navigate to the Recovery Services vault. Select the vault you want to assign the plan to, then go to **Site Recovery | Step 2: Manage Recovery Plans**, as shown in the following screenshot:

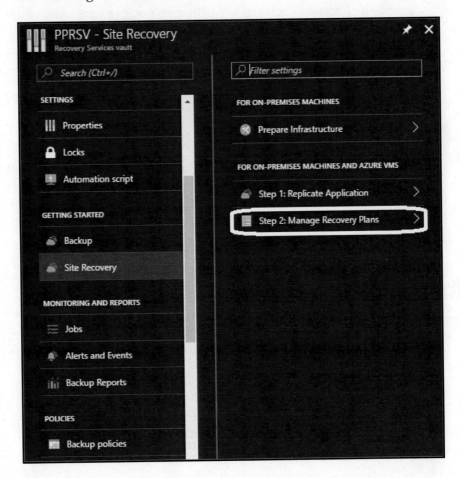

Figure 7.32: Manage recovery plans

2. Once you have clicked on **Step 2: Manage Recovery Plans**, you will be navigated to a new blade, where you need to click on **Recovery plan** to create a new recovery plan.

3. Once you have clicked on **Recovery plan**, you will be navigated to a new blade where you have to specify the following:

    - **Name**: The name of the plan
    - **Source**: Specify the source from which the machines will failover
    - **Target**: Specify the target to which the machines will failover
    - **Allow item with deployment model**: Specify whether the machines will use the classic or resource manager model
    - **Select items**: Specify the VMs that you want to associate with the plan

    Once the recovery plan is created, you can add the following to it:

    - **New groups**: Up to seven recovery plans can be added to the default plan, and they are numbered according to the order you added them in
    - **Manual action**: You can set a manual action that needs to be done by you during the recovery plan process
    - **Script**: You add a script to specify a set of actions that need to be done
    - **Azure runbooks**: You can use Azure runbooks to automate tasks to operate actions during the recovery process

Testing ASR

Before getting started with testing the failover, it is recommended to create a virtual network on which the failover VM will be located.

To test the failover, you have to follow these steps:

1. Navigate to the Recovery Services vault, then go to **Replicated items**, select the VM you want to test the failover for, and then click on **Test Failover**.

2. You will be navigated to a new blade, where you have to specify which virtual network the VM will be located in.

3. Once you have clicked on **OK**, the failover process will start performing the following tasks:
    1. Prerequisites check for test failover.
    2. Creating a test environment.
    3. Creating a test virtual machine.
    4. Preparing the virtual machine.
    5. Starting the virtual machine.
    6. Complete testing: this task will require user interaction by clicking on **Complete testing**.
    7. Cleaning up the test virtual machine.
    8. Cleaning up the test environment.
    9. Finalizing the test failover.

 After *step 5*, the process will stop, so you can check whether the VM is failover to Azure or not, and check whether it is running or not, by visiting the **Virtual Machines** blade. Considering that there will be no public IP address attached to the VM. Therefore, to connect to the VM, you have to attach a public IP address to it. Then, you can get back to the test process and click on **Complete testing**.

Further information

For further information about ASR, you can check out the following links:

- **Multi-tenant support in ASR for replicating VMware virtual machines to Azure through CSP**: https://docs.microsoft.com/en-us/azure/site-recovery/site-recovery-multi-tenant-support-vmware-using-csp

- **Set up disaster recovery to Azure for on-premises physical servers**: https://docs.microsoft.com/en-us/azure/site-recovery/tutorial-physical-to-azure

- **Set up disaster recovery for Hyper-V VMs to your secondary on-premises site**: https://docs.microsoft.com/en-us/azure/site-recovery/tutorial-vmm-to-vmm

- **Set up disaster recovery of on-premises VMware virtual machines or physical servers to a secondary site**: https://docs.microsoft.com/en-us/azure/site-recovery/tutorial-vmware-to-vmware

- **Run a disaster recovery drill to Azure**: https://docs.microsoft.com/en-us/azure/site-recovery/tutorial-dr-drill-azure
- **Run a disaster recovery drill for Hyper-V VMs to your secondary on-premises site**: https://docs.microsoft.com/en-us/azure/site-recovery/tutorial-dr-drill-secondary
- **Failover and failback VMware VMs and physical servers replicated to Azure**: https://docs.microsoft.com/en-us/azure/site-recovery/tutorial-vmware-to-azure-failover-failback

Summary

We are done with the second part of Azure Recovery Services. Throughout the chapter, we have proved the importance of ASR and how to work with it. Therefore, it is very important to check the links that I've provided in the *Further information* section to find out more about it and how to work with things that have not been mentioned in this chapter, such as VMware hosts, and physical servers.

Coming up in the next chapter, you will learn about another solution related to disaster recovery and business continuity, which is called **StorSimple**. You will also learn about some tools that work with Azure, such as AzCopy and Azure Storage Explorer.

8

Extending Your Azure Storage Management

Our journey is coming to an end, and I hope that it has been a beneficial one for you. In this chapter, more information related to Azure Storage management will be covered. Azure StorSimple will be introduced, the reasons for using it, and how to work with it. After that, two of the cool tools for storage management (AzCopy and Azure Storage Explorer) will be covered, and finally, you will be introduced to the three musketeers of Azure Storage: monitoring, diagnosing, and troubleshooting.

In this chapter, the following topics will be covered:

- Azure.StorSimple
- AzCopy
- Azure Storage Explorer
- Azure Storage's three musketeers

Azure StorSimple

Nowadays, we are facing many storage challenges. One of them is rapid data growth that exceeds 40%, which leads to more expense for storage, its protection, and its recovery. **StorSimple** would be a good fit in these scenarios, especially since it spans across on-premises and Azure Cloud, which means you do not have to worry about a storage shortage anymore.

Azure StorSimple is an integrated storage solution. This solution is one of the greatest solutions for managing storage across on-premises devices/hypervisors and Azure Storage. It can manage your primary storage, archival storage, tape backup, and so on. Whatever the type of disk (HDD or SSD), it can manage it. Then, you can assign each part of the storage to the solution that would need it.

There are many reasons for using Azure StorSimple, as stated in the following points:

- **Cost reduction**: According to the current needs, storage will be provided whether from local storage or cloud storage. Moreover, it eliminates redundant data and compresses it.
- **Seamless integration**: StorSimple supports iSCSI and SMB to connect to your data stored on StorSimple, and when connecting, it appears in one location whether it's stored locally or in the cloud.
- **Data mobility**: The existence of the data on Azure supports its accessibility from anywhere. Also, should a disaster occur locally, you can recover your data via another site, or by building a StorSimple cloud appliance on an Azure VM.
- **Easier storage management**: You can manage your storage whether it exists locally or on the cloud, using a single interface that is easy and seamless to use.
- **Simplify data protection and disaster recovery**: Data restoration occurs as needed, which means you do not have to wait too long to get your data recovered. That leads to less downtime, and minimal operational disruption.
- **Higher performance**: As mentioned in previous chapters, there is a premium storage option supported by Microsoft Azure. Using this solution will provide a higher performance and reduced latency.

StorSimple is available in two flavors:

- StorSimple Virtual Array
- StorSimple 8000 series

So, let's bring them to the table and get our hands dirty.

StorSimple Virtual Array

StorSimple Virtual Array manages the storage across on-premises hypervisors and Azure Storage, and it supports Hyper-V 2008 R2 and above, and VMware 5.5 and above.

To implement StorSimple Virtual Array, you have to follow the following steps:

1. First off, navigate to **Marketplace | Storage**, and search for `storsimple virtual`, as shown in the following screenshot:

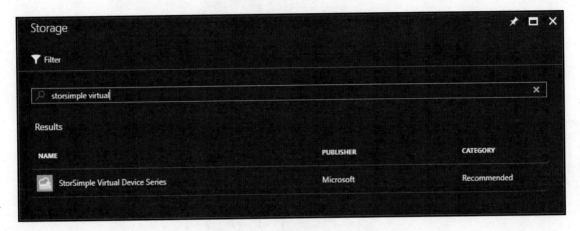

Figure 8.1: Search for StorSimple Virtual Device Series

2. Then, click on **Create**.
3. Once you've clicked on **Create**, a new blade will pop up, asking to fill in the following fields:
   - **Resource name**: The name of the resource
   - **Subscription**: The subscription that will be charged for the service usage
   - **Select a resource group**: The resource group in which the resource will exist
   - **Location**: The region that will host the service

- **Create new Azure storage account**: If you want to create a dedicated storage account for this service, you can tick it, and enter a name for the storage account:

Figure 8.2: Create StorSimple Device Manager

4. Now, you can go back to **More Services**, and search for storsimple, as shown in the following screenshot:

Figure 8.3: Searching for StorSimple Device Managers

5. You will find the **StorSimple Device Manager**, which we created earlier, as shown in the following screenshot:

Figure 8.4: StorSimple Device Managers blade

6. Once you've clicked on the StorSimple Device Manager we have created, a new blade will pop up. Click on **Virtual array**, as shown in the following screenshot:

Figure 8.5: StorSimple Device Manager properties

7. A new blade will pop up, where you can download the virtual array image according to your hypervisor type, as shown in the following screenshot:

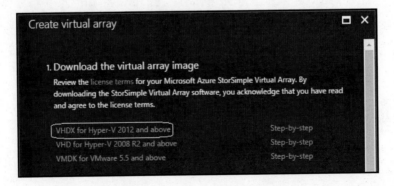

Figure 8.6: Download virtual array image

8. Once the image is downloaded, you can extract it from its ZIP file.

9. Then, head to **Hyper-V** manager and start creating a generation 2 VM with the virtual array image attached to it as the main disk, and 8 GB static RAM.

10. Once the VM is created, navigate to **Settings**, and assign 4 cores for the VM, and a new virtual hard disk to it with at least 500 GB in size.

11. Now, you can start the VM.

12. Once the VM is started and finished with booting, you will be asked to enter a password, and the default is `Password1`.

13. Then, you will be asked to enter a new password.

14. Once done, you will be logged into the VM, as shown in the following screenshot:

Figure 8.7: The StorSimple VM console

15. You can retrieve the NIC information by running the `Get-HcsIpAddress` cmdlet, which will display the following:
    - **The name of the NIC**: It is `Ethernet` by default, and if you have multiple NICs, a number will be added to each additional NIC. For example, `Ethernet1`, `Ethernet2`, and so on.
    - Whether it uses DHCP or not.
    - Whether it is up or down.
    - The IP address.
    - The gateway address.

16. Since it is recommended to use a static IP address for this machine, the following cmdlet will be used:

    ```
    Set-HcsIpAddress -Name Ethernet -IpAddress <The address of the
    VM> -Netmask <The network mask> -Gateway <The gateway address>
    ```

17. Once the IP address is set, you can open a web browser and enter the IP address of the StorSimple VM.

18. The following page will be opened, asking you to enter the password of **StorSimpleAdmin**, which you changed earlier (step 13):

Figure 8.8: StorSimple portal

19. As you can see from the following screenshot, the device is not configured:

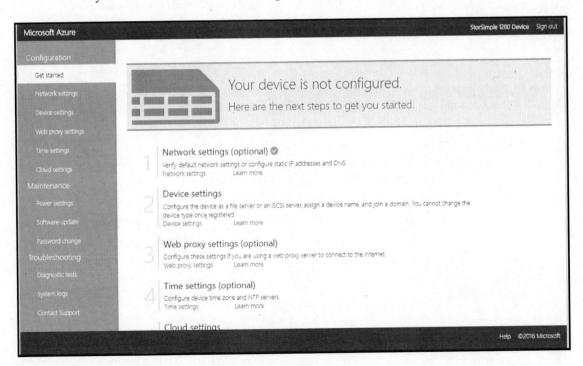

Figure 8.9: Getting started with StorSimple Virtual Array configuration

20. To do so, navigate to **Network settings** to configure the device IP address and DNS, and select whether it will get the IP address automatically or not. Then click on **Apply**, as shown in the following screenshot:

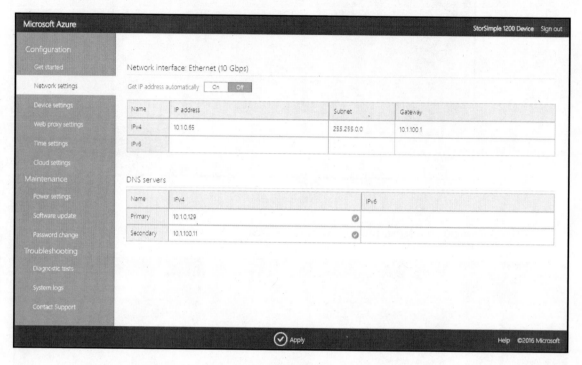

Figure 8.10: Configure the StorSimple network settings

21. After that, navigate to **Device settings** and specify the following:
    - **Device type**: Whether it is a **File server** or **iSCSI server**
    - **Device name**: The name of the device
    - **Join domain**: Select **Yes**, if you want to be domain joined
    - **Domain name**: If you decide to join it to the domain, you have to enter the domain name

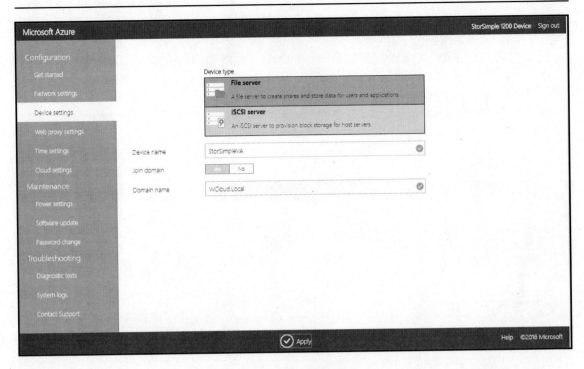

Figure 8.11: Configure device settings

22. Once you've clicked on **Apply**, you will be prompted to enter the domain admin credentials to be able to join the device to the domain, as shown in the following screenshot:

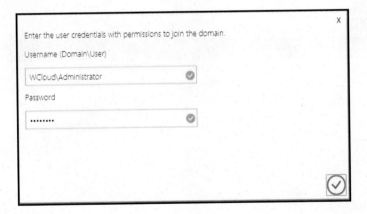

Figure 8.12: Enter the domain admin credentials

23. The next step is to specify whether you have a web proxy or not and if so, you have to enter the following:

- **Web proxy URL**: Enter the web proxy URL
- **Authentication**: Specify the authentication type, whether it is **None** or **Basic**
- **Username**: A user with administrative privilege on the proxy, if authentication is required
- **Password**: The password of the user

Figure 8.13: Configuring web proxy settings

24. Once you've entered the web proxy settings, you have to specify these device **Time settings**:
    - **Time zone**: The time zone in which the device exists
    - **Primary NTP server**: The time server with which it will sync time
    - **Secondary NTP server** (optional): Another NTP server, in case the first one faced a downtime issue

Figure 8.14: Time settings configurations

25. Then you have to specify your **Cloud settings**, which require a service registration key for the device if this is your first time, as shown in the following screenshot:

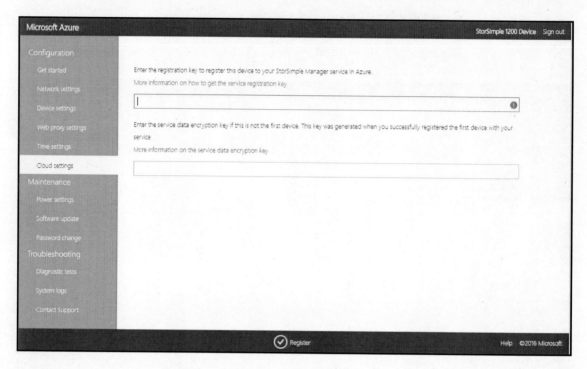

Figure 8.15: Configure cloud settings

26. To get that key, you have to navigate again to the Azure portal, then go to **StorSimple Device Manager** and open the device manager that was created earlier. Then click on **Keys**, as shown in the following screenshot:

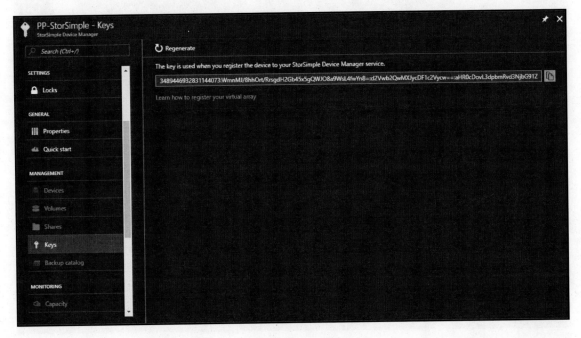

Figure 8.16: Retrieving the key

27. Once the key is copied, you can paste it into the **Cloud settings**, and click on **Register**, as shown in the following screenshot:

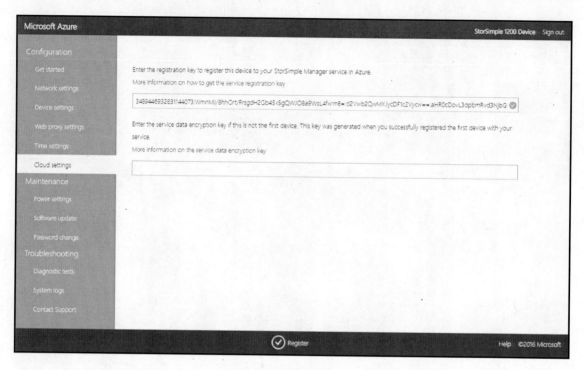

Figure 8.17: Registering cloud settings

28. Once done, a **Service Data Encryption Key** will pop up, as shown in the following screenshot:

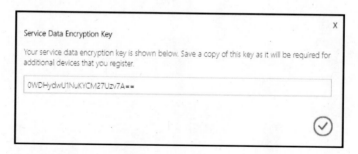

Figure 8.18: Service Data Encryption Key

You have to save a copy of that key, as it will be used when registering additional devices.

29. So far, you are done with the device configurations on that portal.

30. Navigate again to the Azure portal, then go to **StorSimple Device Manager** and open the device manager that has been created earlier. Then click on **Devices**, as shown in the following screenshot:

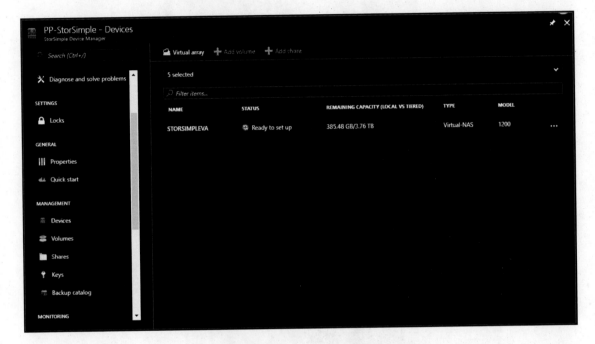

Figure 8.19: Device management on Azure portal

31. By now, you will have noted that the **STATUS** of the device is **Ready to set up**, so we will click on it, and a new blade will pop up.

32. To configure it, click on **Configure**, and a new blade will pop up, asking to specify the following:

- **Cloud storage encryption**: It is recommended to enable the encryption
- **Encryption key**: You have to enter a 32-character encryption key
- **Confirm encryption key**: Enter the encryption key again, as shown in the following screenshot:

Figure 8.20: Configure StorSimple Virtual Array

33. Then, we will click on **Storage account credentials** to configure it too, and if there are no storage account credentials already added, add them as shown in the following screenshot:

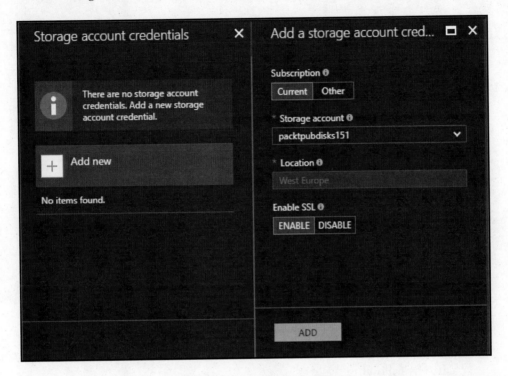

Figure 8.21: Configure storage account credentials

34. Once done, click on **ADD**, then click on **Configure**.

35. Once the configuration is done, you can navigate to **Shares**, and click on **Add share**, as shown in the following screenshot:

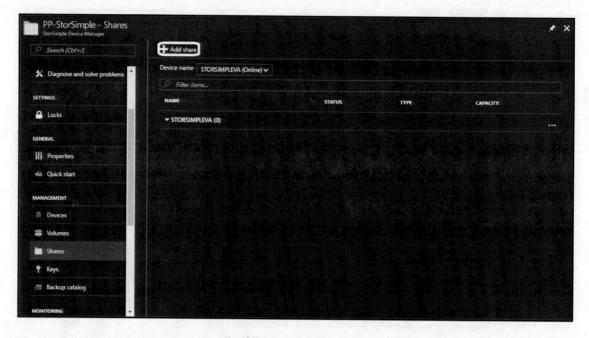

Figure 8.22: Shares on the StorSimple device

36. Once you've clicked on **Add share**, a new blade will pop up, where you have to specify the following:
    - **Select device**: If you have multiple devices, you can select the device on which you want to create this share
    - **Share name**: The name of the share
    - **Description**: Describe the share for more illustration
    - **Type**: There are two types:
        - **Locally pinned**: It will create a thickly-provisioned file share on the StorSimple file server on-premises, and does not span to the cloud, and it is commonly used for applications that need low latency and higher performance
        - **Tiered**: It creates a thin file share that provisions 10% of on-premises, and 90% to the cloud

- **Capacity**: The size of the file share
- **Set default full permission to**: Specify the user who will be able to access the file share

Figure 8.23: Create a file share

37. Once the file share is created, you can access it from on-premises, as shown in the following screenshot:

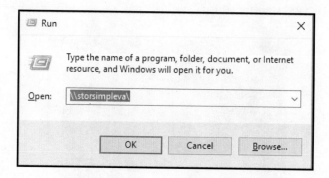

Figure 8.24: Opening the file share

38. You will be prompted to enter the credentials of the user with permissions to that file share.

39. Once the credentials are entered, you can access the file, as shown in the following screenshot:

Figure 8.25: Accessing the file share

StorSimple 8000 series

Unlike StorSimple Virtual Array, **StorSimple 8000 series** is a SAN solution with affordable cost and some amazing features. StorSimple 8000 series supports only iSCSI to connect to it and it does not support SMB, which means you cannot create file shares on it.

This device can only span storage from the data center to Azure, and no other cloud providers. Once you purchase the appliance, you have to check the following links to implement it with no issues:

- **Review safety**: `https://docs.microsoft.com/en-us/azure/storsimple/storsimple-8000-safety`
- **Unpack, rack, cable an 8100**: `https://docs.microsoft.com/en-us/azure/storsimple/storsimple-8100-hardware-installation`
- **Unpack, rack, cable an 8600**: `https://docs.microsoft.com/en-us/azure/storsimple/storsimple-8600-hardware-installation`
- **Supported hardware for the 10 GbE network interfaces on your StorSimple device**: `https://docs.microsoft.com/en-us/azure/storsimple/storsimple-supported-hardware-for-10-gbe-network-interfaces`

 For more information about StorSimple 8000 series administration, you can check the following link: `https://docs.microsoft.com/en-us/azure/storsimple/storsimple-8000-manager-service-administration`.

AzCopy

AzCopy is a command-line tool that is used for copying data to and from Azure Storage Blob, File, and Table services, or to and from objects within the same storage account, and even between different storage accounts.

AzCopy is available in two flavors:

- AzCopy on Windows
- AzCopy on Linux

- You can download AzCopy for Windows from the following link: `http://az837173.vo.msecnd.net/azcopy-6-3-0/MicrosoftAzureStorageTools.msi`
- You can download AzCopy for Linux from the following link: `https://azcopy.azureedge.net/azcopy-6-0-0-netcorepreview/azcopy_6.0.0_netcorepreview_all.tar.gz`
- AzCopy on Linux works for macOS too.

The installation of AzCopy is very straightforward, and once it is installed you have to navigate to its installation path to be able to run its commands. Working with AzCopy is very easy and the data move process can be executed smoothly.

Uploading a folder to Azure Blob

To upload a folder to Azure Blob, you need to run the following command:

```
AzCopy /source:C:\FolderX\ /Dest:<BlobServiceEndpoint/The container you
want to upload the file to> /DestKey:/<The Storage account key>
```

Downloading an Azure Blob service container

To download a container from Azure Blob container, you need to run the following command:

```
azcopy /source:<Blob Service Container Endpoint> /Dest:C:\FolderX
/Sourcekey:/<The Storage account key> /S
```

Where /S is the recursive mode option, it will download all the objects that exist in the blob.

- For further information about AzCopy commands on Windows, you can check the following link: https://docs.microsoft.com/en-us/azure/storage/common/storage-use-azcopy
- For further information about AzCopy commands on Linux, you can check the following link: https://docs.microsoft.com/en-us/azure/storage/common/storage-use-azcopy-linux

Azure Storage Explorer

Azure Storage Explorer is a simple application for managing Azure Storage. It is easy to work with, and is available for Windows, Linux, and macOS. Currently, Azure Storage Explorer is still in preview.

You can download Azure Storage Explorer from the following link, and you only need to specify your OS to download a compatible version: `https://azure.microsoft.com/en-us/features/storage-explorer/`.

Connecting to Azure Storage using Azure Storage Explorer

Once Azure Storage Explorer is installed, and you have opened it, you will be prompted to specify how you want to connect to your storage.

There are three ways to connect:

- Add an Azure account, specifying Azure environment (Azure, Azure China, Azure Germany, Azure US Government, Azure Stack)
- Use a connection string or shared access signature URI
- Use the storage account name and key

- For more information about connection strings, you can check the following link: `https://docs.microsoft.com/en-us/azure/storage/common/storage-configure-connection-string`
- For more information about shared access signature, you can check the following link: `https://docs.microsoft.com/en-us/azure/storage/common/storage-dotnet-shared-access-signature-part-1`

To connect to the storage in an Azure account perform the following steps:

1. Select the first option, then click on **Sign in...,** as demonstrated in the following screenshot:

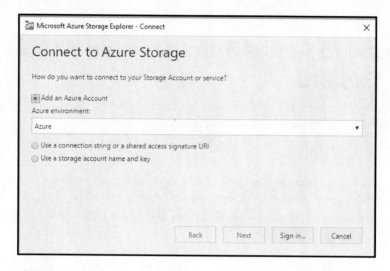

Figure 8.26: Connect to Azure Storage

2. Once you've clicked on **Sign in...,** you will be prompted to enter your Azure account credentials.
3. Then, navigate to **Manage accounts** to specify the subscription/s you want to manage, as shown in the following screenshot:

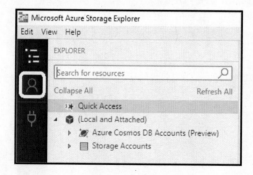

Figure 8.27: Navigate to manage accounts

4. Once navigated, you need to specify the subscriptions, as shown in the following screenshot:

Figure 8.28: Selecting the subscriptions

5. Then, the storage accounts that exist in that subscription will be displayed, as shown in the following screenshot:

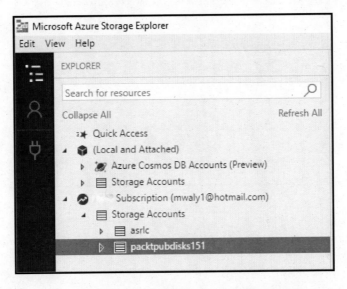

Figure 8.29: Storage accounts that exist in the subscription that has been selected

6. You can also connect to **Azure Cosmos DB Accounts (Preview)**, as shown in the following screenshot:

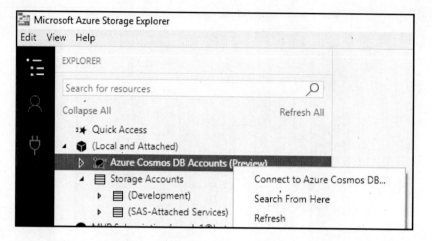

Figure 8.30: Connect to Azure Cosmos DB

7. Next, you need to select the API (**DocumentDB**, **Table**, **Graph**, **MongoDB**) and enter its connection string, as shown in the following screenshot:

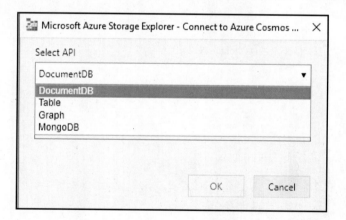

Figure 8.31: Selecting the API

 For more information about Cosmos DB, you can check the following link: https://docs.microsoft.com/en-us/azure/cosmos-db/introduction.

Managing Azure Storage accounts using Azure Storage Explorer

As mentioned earlier, Azure Storage Explorer is used for managing Azure Storage. With Azure Storage Explorer, you can create/remove Azure Storage services, download/upload storage, and so on.

Creating an Azure Storage service

Creating an Azure Storage service is very straightforward. Navigate to the storage account you want to create a storage service within, right-click on the service, for example, **Blob Containers**. Then, select **Create Blob Container** as shown in the following screenshot:

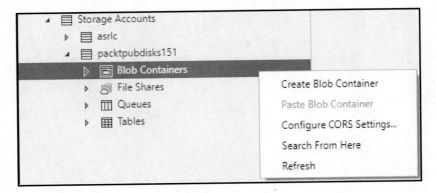

Figure 8.32: Create an Azure Storage service

To manage a specific blob container/file share, you have to hover over it and double-click on it, and a new console will open with the tasks that can be done with it, as shown in the following screenshots:

Figure 8.33: Managing a blob container

Figure 8.34: Managing a Queue

The same goes for the table service, as shown in the following screenshot:

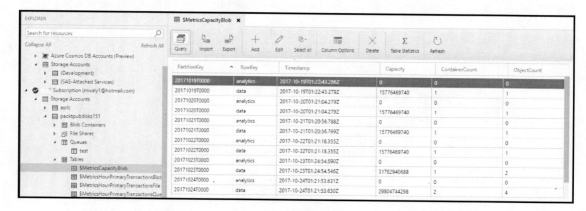

Figure 8.35: Managing Tables

Azure Storage's three musketeers

Facing issues while working with an application/VM that works on Azure because of Azure Storage would be painful. Therefore, to avoid such a scenario, you should monitor your environment properly, diagnose the issue, and troubleshoot it once it occurs. And there's the three musketeers that will save your day: monitoring, diagnosing, and troubleshooting.

To monitor your storage services, you have to navigate to your storage account and select its metrics to display the monitored metrics, as shown in the following screenshot:

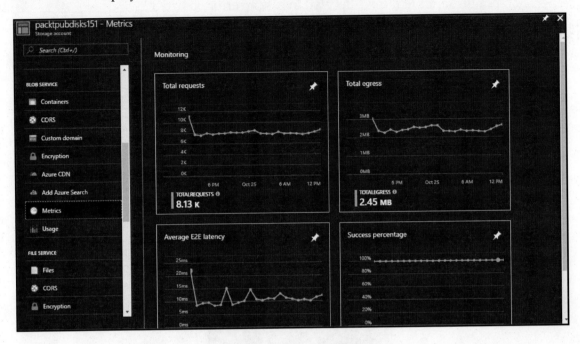

Figure 8.36: Display Blob storage service metrics

You can also add alerts, in case a metric exceeded a threshold set by you. To do so, you have to navigate to the storage account that you want to monitor, scroll down to **Alert rules**, and click on **Add alert.** A new blade will pop up, where you will need to fill in the following fields:

- **Resource**: Select the resource the alert rule is on. For example, Table service.
- **Name**: The name of the alert.
- **Description**: The description of the alert.
- **Metric**: Select the metric that you want this alert rule to monitor.
- **Condition**: Specify whether it will be greater than, less than, and so on.
- **Period**: Select a time span during which to monitor the metric data specified by this alert rule.

- **Email owners, contributors, and readers**: Tick it if you want to email the owners, contributors, and readers of this service. You can also add additional administrators to receive the alert in case an error occurred.

Figure 8.37: Creating an alert

Issues happen and you will need to diagnose these issues to avoid any downtime and huge impact on your solution. Therefore, you need to be aware of the following:

- Adding baseline values to your metrics based on which you can specify what cause this issue
- The errors generated from the application itself, that would appear in its logs
- The users' reports that the application is not functioning properly
- There are some issues with Azure Storage services

Based on your monitoring and diagnosing, you have to start troubleshooting. The following URL covers how to troubleshoot most of the common errors: `https://docs.microsoft.com/en-us/azure/storage/common/storage-monitoring-diagnosing-troubleshooting#troubleshooting-guidance`.

Summary

This chapter has covered some of the coolest tools that can be used with Azure Storage. You can read the articles by clicking on the links provided for more information.

It's been a fruitful journey talking about Azure Storage, why you should use it, and how to work with it in different scenarios. I hope you have gained the knowledge you need from this book, and I'd like to thank you for reading it.

Index